MW00439227

Almost Jewish

Blinkquen

Also by Chad Felix Greene

Children's Titles

What's That Thing on Your Head?

How's That Thing Stay on Your Head?

Ronni, The Little Jewish Girl Who Loved Israel

8 Things You Can Do To Make God Smile Everyday

Almost Jewish

Converting to Judaism, the Hard Way

Chad Felix Greene

Blinkquen

Almost Jewish

ISBN: 9781521231708

Imprint: Independently published

www.chadfelixgreene.com

First Edition

Printing 2017

Printed in the United State of America

To my Jewish Family: Ronni Fox-Glaser and Norman Glaser who taught me what being Jewish really is and who loved me when I needed it most.

To Rabbi Jean Eglinton who didn't just help me across the finish line, but opened new doors of possibilities in Judaism I had not considered. She has been a lifeline when I was in need, spiritually and in my life. I am grateful to her beyond my ability to express it.

To my friends Christina, Mike and Janna who lived through every step and always found Chanukah themed presents no matter the occasion.

Contents

Preface

I am *almost* Jewish. Well, I am Jewish. I am Jewish *now* I mean. I wasn't Jewish last Monday, but today I am Jewish[1]. When I began writing this book I was not Jewish yet; but wasn't quite *not* Jewish either. I was *almost* Jewish. I spent a decade – yes, an actual decade – living as a Jew, identifying as a Jew and taking my sweet time along the road to Jewish conversion. This is what this book is about actually. I did not begin in a typical fashion and I certainly did not take the road mostly traveled either. I'm not really sure if I should be the one giving advice on this, but here I am. This book is so that ten years from now *you* are not in the same boat I have been in for the entirety of my adult life[2]. I want for you to *be* Jewish and not just *feel* Jewish. (Note the Jewish sentence structure, write this down)[3] I want for you to know with confidence that you have chosen a life that has meaning for you and not just an interesting identity that goes along with some vague concept that you really like bagels.

I want you to know what you are doing *before* you put on the kippah[4] and go too far down the social line of calling yourself *Jewish.* You can't be kind of pregnant and you can't be kind of Jewish. It's very black and white kids; don't let Rabbi So-and-so tell you otherwise on the internet. There is a process and some expectations. Those expectations vary from rabbi to rabbi but they follow a similar path and timeline. There are many books focused on that topic alone and while I kind of find myself explaining how the process works, I really just want to give you an idea. The best way to do that is to really just show you what I have experienced. If you decide to convert after reading this then you've earned it. No. Seriously.

Like I said, there are many books on converting to Judaism but this one will tell you the truth about what goes on behind the scenes. I have lived in the limbo of "Ger" (it's what you are when you are converting) for a decade now and I can tell you many things to avoid and how to take a much easier path than I chose. Hopefully I will make you laugh a bit too. I am a very funny guy. Ask anyone. My style is story telling from my own experience with bits and pieces tossed out to you as they feel appropriate.

Just so we are clear, I am not now nor do I ever plan to be a building-bridges Chanukah-Bush[5] hippie Jew. I technically classify myself as Conservative[6] only because I cannot be Orthodox and I am not really Reform. I have strong opinions and I'm not afraid to use them. (Requirement #472 of being Jewish) But I am open to the reality that we all find out path in unique ways. You should not feel that my perspective on a topic is the best one. I think it is the best one, but you don't have to. You really don't need anything other than a curious interest to feel as though this book speaks to you.

Look, taking on this process is not easy. It is not fancy or nice or pretty. Jews are a very unique and diverse group of people and you really do not have any idea what you are doing. In fact, you should probably skim through about half of this book and maybe choose something more suitable like Wicca instead.

Just a suggestion.

Introduction

People can convert to Judaism? It's not all that surprising really to find out many people do not know this. In some of my earlier discussions I had several people tell me that they just didn't think it was possible at all. Judaism is a strange religion to the outside world in many ways as hopefully my stories will demonstrate. I have found people rarely understand anything about it yet feel as though they do.

People assume Judaism is just the first half of Christianity or is in some way a partner religion with Islam[7]. Casual observers notice the difference between an Orthodox Jew and the Jewish guy who works a few cubicles down but they assume they are both exactly the same.

The things so many find puzzling utterly baffle me now looking back. But I do remember how it felt to pick up my first book on Jewish conversion[8] and I remember the anticipation I experienced flipping through the pages.

I can't say it fully prepared me, but it did give me hope that I could really do this if I wanted to. Anyone can change their religion. Judaism is unique, however, in that you must follow a path to do so. This path changes from one movement to another but a general rule stands that you must have the approval of a rabbi before you can become Jewish[9]. This isn't really a faith you can adopt on your own.

Throughout the following chapters I guide you through my own history and the various observations I have found. I enjoy a mixture of biographical storytelling and direct "how to" instruction. I like to summarize things and provide my own definitions and I am sure everyone will find them horribly inaccurate and offensive but they are mine and I stand by them![10] At the end of the book I will include notes clarifying details indicated in the text by a number. Please reference if you get stuck on a word or concept.[11]

As much as I encourage you through my own mistakes and advice, I do hope you will find a way to bring yourself to this process as much as you can. It can be so easy to be overwhelmed and I think you should take it a step at a time. Hopefully me telling you how I did it can provide you with some comfort that at least you won't make the same mistakes I did.

At the end of this book I list some helpful books to help you on your way. There is a standard to conversion but it is expressed in endless variety and I really shouldn't be your only example. No, really. Thank you for allowing me to share myself with you.

Almost Jewish

1

In the Beginning There Was an Oy

I'd be lying if I said I always felt Jewish[12]. Hell, I didn't even know what a Jew was until I was about 10 or 11. But I do remember being fascinated by the characters in the Bible and wanting to be just like them. I was a Baptist/Pentecostal mutt and I was also a very weird loner type kid. What nine-year-old reads the Bible on the weekends and then spends three hours listening to his crazy great-aunt tell him about how Angels and Demons had a battle earlier that morning in the sky and believes her?

I'm just sayin'.

I was utterly fascinated with my religion back then, but something felt out of place. I mean didn't Jesus study with Rabbis?[13] He didn't have a Christmas tree or anything but he was Jewish. Why wasn't I Jewish too? I soon discovered that while Jews were in the Bible and Jesus was actually Jewish, actual Jewish people were to be shunned. You see the Jews both rejected and killed Jesus and even though they knew he was G-d's[14] son they still did those things.[15]

My Jewish curiosity ended there and would not resurface until I was 19.

Jump forward to age 19.

Is this where I found myself walking into a Synagogue and feeling an overwhelming tug to the glowing Torah scrolls at the front? No. Actually, it started while channel surfing and catching a live broadcast of thousands of Jews dancing in full dress singing praises to someone called 'Yeshua', whom I quickly learned meant "Jesus." (It means Joshua, but now is not the time for silly technicalities)[16]

"The Jews found Jesus." I thought. *"Hmm, well I'll be."*

That really was my response.

To give you a general idea of what happened to me from age 10 to 19 I can summarize it as such: I became a Jesus Freak[17] before being one was cool, grew my hair down to my shoulders, planned for a future in Pastoral studies at Liberty University, then the gay got me, terribly traumatic fall from grace, Wicca was involved, bam I'm 19.

I had resigned myself to being a liberal Christian, you know the kind where Hell is optional and Jesus is some kind of hippie who walks around petting bunnies and being vegan wearing cruelty-free organic robes, but this sudden shock to my worldview sent me back to my earlier curiosity towards Jews. My Jesus Freak days taught me that once the

Jews accepted Jesus that the end of the world was soon to be upon us. Well, technically *my* Christianity told me it would be sort of in the middle of the world ending, but I wasn't about to get all specific. I called my best friend and breathlessly announced what I was sure was a stunning discovery of this great event in world history. (I actually thought I had witnessed live the widespread conversion of Jews to Christianity…it's in the book of Revelation people!)

My friend calmly informed me that no, he was pretty sure Jews had not accepted Jesus in mass; otherwise there would be something on the news. I protested that yes it was true when on TV at that very moment the announcer quelled my enthusiasm with a message about their ministries reaching out to Jews around the world. *"Oh."* I said with disappointment. I mean how often do you instantly believe the world is going to end and find out it's not in the same hour?

But it sparked curiosity in me again and I began trying to find out about these Jews I kept hearing about and why some of them called Jesus "Yeshua." I still wasn't sure exactly what they did or where they were, but I intended to find out. I did so by renting movies from Blockbuster, (remember Blockbuster?) that fell under the category "Jewish."

Then one evening I came upon a title called *School Days* with Brendan Frazier about a Jewish boy in the 1950's

I believe who wanted to go to an Ivy League school but had to pretend he wasn't Jewish.

Something struck a chord.

Something struck a chord very loudly.

Being as I was to the inclination of multiple spiritual paths, I began exploring the idea that maybe I had been Jewish in a past life. With my trusty Sylvia Browne tape in hand I prepared myself for a past life regression to see and find out.[18] Sure enough I found myself as a 19-year-old young man named Jacob Greene who was flying a plane in the 1940's and crashed into the ocean.[19] I had a significant feeling that I had put a great deal of effort into hiding my Jewish identity so that I could be accepted. The last thing I remember is ripping off my Star-of-David necklace and watching it float above my head under water.

Good enough for me.

I decided that very moment that I would find a way to be Jewish in this life so that I could repair the damage I did in my last life with abandoning and hiding my faith. It was March and I was 19, I had an absolutely overwhelming desire to become Jewish. I wasn't even sure it was possible. I had to keep it a secret though. My poor family already had to deal with me and the gay thing, adding Jewish on top of it surely would result in death of some kind. I did a quick internet search and I found a book called: *Choosing a Jewish Life* by Anita Diamant and I ordered it.

The day I got it I read the entire thing.

Even though it felt incredibly complicated and in depth I felt sure I could do it. I walked around thinking to myself for days, *"Am I really going to do this? Am I really going to become Jewish??"*

The resounding answer was *yes.*

It really did happen that way. Don't judge me.

2

Coming Home...Well Sort of

I think I gave myself exactly one week before I felt prepared and brave enough to go to the local Synagogue and approach the Rabbi. I hadn't exactly figured out my cover story yet but I was pretty sure *"Hey Rabbi, while doing a past life regression after watching this movie..."* was going to get a door slammed in my face. But I had mentally committed so strongly that I felt I couldn't turn back. I would just think of something.

I found the giant building thanks to the internet but for the life of me I could not find an entrance that worked. The Synagogue had these giant doors, but they were locked. There was also a side door but it was locked too. There was no large sign out front with a catchy slogan with missing letters or anything. Confused, I paced back and forth and then discovered a little buzzer with faded instructions to use it if I wanted to get in.

I did.

A few minutes later a very annoyed older gentleman in a beard opened the door partway and tilted his head. I said: *"Hello, my name is Chad and I just read this book about converting to Judaism and I would really like to see if I could talk to you and…"* With an outstretched palm in the *"stop in the name of love"* fashion and a nod the man, who had identified himself as the Rabbi (he didn't have a black hat or curly sideburns so I wasn't sure) muttered something about coming to services and then he'd see and then he shut the door.

I stood there utterly crestfallen.

Here I had just spent a very stressful week working up the nerve to come here and I was certain I had expressed what should have been interpreted as enthusiasm to the man and he rejected me. I knew from the book that a Rabbi was supposed to reject you three times to test your sincerity[20], but I assumed it would involve you finishing your sentence. Embarrassed and defeated I found my way back to my car and I felt like crying but I decided that all hope was not lost. I would just go to a service like he said and then I was sure he would talk to me.

He didn't talk to me for seven years. But we'll get to that.

That following Friday I came in for the evening service and let me tell you that was no easy task. First of all, synagogues do not always have a convenient sign outside as I discovered when I first tried to enter the building. They don't ring bells, announce their services on the radio or hand out fliers.[21] I decided that 6pm was a good average time for church services to start in general and I knew Friday was the day and not Sunday! I showed up too early and ended up sitting in a pew for 45 minutes waiting for something to happen.

What was my first experience in a synagogue like? Insightful? Beautiful? Inspiring? Like coming home?

Nope.

It looked exactly like a church.

It had rows and rows of pews flowing down an angled floor to a stage with a pulpit. Behind the pulpit was a large curtain and a hanging light with a replica of the Ten Commandments at the top. The ceiling was massive and domed with giant stained glass art.[22] I sat near the front and waited with anticipation for the thrill of remembering and a deep spiritual awakening that was sure to overwhelm me and bring me to joyous tears.

Nothing.

When the six other people finally showed up and the organ began to play I knew I had miscalculated something in my plan.

The service was…interesting.

Coming from a charismatic background I was unaccustomed to the drone of call and repeat reading, and sleepy singing in a language I did not know. I was bored out of my mind and a little more than just disappointed.

I was also confused.

First of all, nothing was sacrificed.

I know that sounds ridiculous but I was anticipating an animal sacrifice[23] like the felt board demonstrations had promised me. Also, I had built up an inner monologue about being open minded about the whole animal sacrifice thing which I was morally opposed to. I figured someone would explain it to me. Second, all the things we read were little more than Hallmark card snippets about loving one another and blah blah world peace.[24] There was no fearsome deity ready to smite the masses. No tales of Abraham holding a dagger above Jacob, no enthusiastic declarations and pleas for a Messiah, no mention of Jesus at all. I assumed they would at least mention something about not believing in Jesus.[25]

The Torah part was kind of neat though. I had been anticipating what was behind that curtain (animal sacrifices naturally). In a church, you just never know. It could be a big pool for baptisms or it could be filled with pictures or have a big cross or anything. The curtain protected several brightly decorated and very large scrolls and the ceremony of dismantling the chosen scroll was kind of exciting. Upon rolling it out I did sit up in my seat a bit in anticipation, but so far Hebrew had not resonated with my soul. The reading was fast and over too soon. Suddenly the scroll was put away and they were handing out little plastic cups of wine.

In church, we always used grape juice.

I was so confused.

Also, there was a lot of work going on and everybody drove. This was Friday night, wasn't there this whole Sabbath thing?[26] The word was brought up, but I just didn't get it. Afterwards everybody walked into a very large room with a table full of food.[27] Now I was a W.A.S.P. with a little bit of soul[28] and you don't just walk up to a table full of food and eat it while visiting someplace new.

Big mistake.

Two older ladies there quickly found me trying to blend into the wall and I soon found myself surrounded with plates of cookies and cheese and a flurry of questions.

"Are you Jewish?"

"Do you go to school?

"Are you in Rabbis' class?"

"Are you single?"

I was overwhelmed. I managed to escape the uncomfortable food thing and I tried to explain that I fully intended on converting to Judaism. They seemed more interested in my career plans. Meanwhile I was waiting for the Rabbi to make an appearance so I could talk to him. Pastors always make rounds so I assumed he would too. I mean what religious leader doesn't welcome newcomers right? He did finally appear but walked right past me and went for the food. He kept talking to other people so I couldn't find a window to jump in. Also, I was fighting off old ladies with plates of cookies. After several attempts to get his attention I finally decided it was a lost cause and I scurried away while the ladies were distracted. But one younger woman did approach me.

She and I talked and I asked questions and she patiently listened and answered them. I rambled on and on about Christianity as I was intensely curious about contrasting what I assumed was two parts of the same religion.

She had never heard any of it.

When I said, *"So why didn't anyone mention Jesus?"* she said, *"Why would we talk about him?"*

I will never know how this woman kept a straight face and stayed so kind.

3

New Jew

After being rescued from my unpleasant and disillusioning experience, I temporarily felt a new confidence that even if I didn't get things right away they would eventually come to me. I returned to the synagogue three more times but each time I experienced the same rejection from the Rabbi. Surpassing the "three times" rule I finally decided that he must just not like me. During this time, however, I had begun enthusiastically imagining myself as being Jewish. I admit that trying to remember now is difficult as one memory in April of that year jumps to my next memory in August, but I know that somehow in that time period I developed a very strong confidence in my newfound spiritual identity.

But there was trouble afoot.

In my three visits, I had spent about an hour afterwards talking with my one and only friend at the synagogue and I had come to rely on her encouragement since she was the sole person in my world who knew what I was doing. For some reason, however, I felt a strong desire to convince her that I had a great network of support from friends and family. I think I read that some Rabbis won't convert you if you abandon your family and I didn't want to break any rules. I just figured I would sort it all out on my own later.

So, in one particular discussion my new friend was driving me back to my car which happened to be parked in front of one of my friend's parent's house. I was fairly close to their son and had grown to know them well. Somewhere I read that there was a tradition where someone made you a blanket to welcome you into the Jewish faith (I have never heard of it since) but I was sure this would be a clear sign that I was proving myself worthy of Jewishness to my new friend. In my rambling, I lied and to the question, *"So is your family supporting you in this?"* I said, *"Oh yeah, even my friend's mom who lives right here is so excited she is making me this insert name I can't remember blanket."*

I had no reason to believe this would blow up in my face.

And then the mom walked outside to investigate the mysterious car idling in the road in front of her house. My heart stopped but I tried to play it cool. She was confused as to why I was sitting in a woman's car at almost 10pm and in an attempt to lighten things up my new friend said, *"Oh, I hear you are very supportive of Chad's decision to convert to Judaism!"*

Not in on my little scam, the mom replied, *"Oh? This is the first I am hearing of it."*

Then they both looked at me and I said, *"Well, it's about time for me to go home now!"*

Embarrassed beyond belief I think I said something like *"That's strange, we just talked about it."* And being polite my new friend dismissed it as well with an *"I'm surprised she reacted so shocked."*

I wasn't getting out of it that easily. I really hadn't meant to *lie* lie. I was furiously discussing many things and chose to throw in what I assumed would eventually be true (and it was in fact eventually true outside of the blanket thing).

I learned a valuable lesson.

On the other hand, I was too humiliated to face her again, now convinced she would tell everyone I was a liar. I didn't go back to the synagogue for months. Convinced I had ruined any chance of being a part of that community, I decided to go on with this Jewish thing my own way. I figured I could read my way through it. How hard could it be? I did the same thing with Wicca, didn't I? The problem was that the books never mentioned how one was to deal with their brand new Jewish identity in terms of discussing it with others. Well, they did, but it all sounded so very *'How to talk about your alcohol problem with family and friends.'* Here is a good time to pay attention because you're going to learn from my mistakes, my many, many mistakes.

Jewish identity and Jewish religious practice are separate things. Unlike Christianity, you cannot just declare yourself Jewish by pure will alone. Unfortunately, I refused to acknowledge this and was convinced I could do this my own way. My first stumbling block was figuring out how to simultaneously inform my friends of my new religion while keeping it quiet from my family. I told my friends who shrugged, and with good reason, this was probably my third or fourth new religion in so many months. But I persisted and being good 20-somethings they agreed to refer to me as "Jewish" from then on.

I was thrilled when I met a friend of my friend who said, *"Oh, you're his Jewish friend right?"*

Score!

Avoiding actual Jewish people at all costs fearing they had all learned of my treachery and would rebuke me in some secret Jewish way if they found out, I started walking a very shaky line where I was Jewish to non-Jews but actual Jews had never heard of me. This has a name by the way, it's a Pseudo-Jew[29]. Interestingly there are people who go around pretending to be Jewish without any connection to Judaism or any interest. I felt this did not apply to me because I genuinely wanted to be Jewish, I just didn't feel comfortable going about it the normal way. Also, the Rabbi wouldn't talk to me.

I would spend the next nine years with this self-imposed fear.

My first public Jewish experience came when I got a seasonal job at a bookstore in the mall. Now at this time in my life I felt that the best way to gain equality for whatever I felt oppressed over was to shout as loud as possible and threaten to sue if I felt offended. Armed with two handy-dandy socially acceptable minority labels I marched into my interview wearing an obnoxiously large series of paper-Mache crumpled balls painted like the rainbow. It was attached to my belt and kind of looked like I was wearing a string of golf balls.

Proud of my personal fight for freedom I informed the interviewer that I intended to wear this symbol of pride every day and it would be illegal for her to prevent me (wrong, actually). I also informed her that I would not be working Friday nights or Saturday mornings or any Jewish holiday. She stuttered with a, *"uh uh, I will have to see with the manager…"*

Somehow, I got hired. Ironically it was for the night shift in which my job was to organize the store and shelve books with about five other employees, all of whom were unimpressed with my brave display of gay pride against an oppressive culture. My request for Fridays and Saturdays off was denied as well because of scheduling. I accepted it as my first real taste of discrimination because of my faith but I soldiered on.

I was newly 20, fearless and determined to be a complete pain in everyone's ass.

It wasn't intentional, I blame TV.

For the record the string of balls lasted exactly the first night before I realized a) no actual customer would ever see it and even give me the opportunity to be discriminated against so I could stand up for myself and b) it really got in the way of all of my climbing and moving.

The store manager was curious about me, however, seeing me as a free spirit. She complimented me on being fearless and creative and liked that I was converting to Judaism. While she couldn't give me the days off I requested, she certainly supported my choice and she asked me about it all the time. Since I was not going to a synagogue or speaking with a Rabbi, I just had to BS my way around her questions.

This experience made me realize that telling people I was converting to Judaism was far more complicated than it needed to be. I soon quit and got hired at a call center where I decided I would avoid this "converting" mess altogether and just pretend I had always been Jewish.

I considered this to be a good and reasonable plan.

My logic was this: When one converts to Judaism they are treated, and considered to be as if they were born Jewish. This means I have the right to re-write my life as if I were Jewish. I mean what could possibly go wrong with this plan? The first day of training I waited like a hunting lion prepared to pounce at the very first opportunity I could find to announce my various orientations. This came easy because on the first day everybody goes around the table and introduces themselves. I took this opportunity to say, *"Hello, I'm Chad, I'm 20 and I'm Gay and Jewish."*

*crickets

I quietly applauded myself for my fearless smack in the face to the establishment and then proceeded to engage in every single conversation with things like, *"Oh, you like pizza? I'm Jewish so I can't have sausage"* and *"Customer service experience? Well Gays are often discriminated against in the workplace, in fact…"* By the end of training no one would make eye contact or speak to me. I assumed it was their obvious bigotry in action. I planned to complain to HR about how uncomfortable I was with their hostility. Flush with the successful rendering of my pretend life, I moved into the real job post-training with a smug satisfaction that I had built the life I wanted. They would never be the wiser and this would really make me Jewish. I forgot that a high school friend's mother who had known me since I was a toddler also worked there. A good rule for those trying to fabricate an entirely new life story: Don't do it around people who know people who know you.

Before I could contain it suddenly everyone knew I had been viciously lying. It was awkward for a few days but then it calmed down and along with my obsessive insistence that I was too Jewish, soon those annoyed by my lies ignored me and those who believed me liked me.

Oh to be 20 again.

That job lasted exactly two months and I finally just left.

Pretending to have always been Jewish wasn't working either.[30] It was far too difficult and it's not like I was in the Witness Protection Program. I decided my only choice was to go by the tried and true rule of not bringing it up unless somebody asks, and then just be honest…which I shall be doing for the rest of my natural life it seems.

Rounding out my one year anniversary of deciding to become Jewish caused me to reevaluate my plan. Clearly this independent thing wasn't working, my family had dismissed it, my friends thought it was cute and I didn't know enough about Judaism to pull off acting like I was Jewish.

I needed Jews!

The problem was, I was scared to death of them.

Look. After a solid year of saying the phrase *'I'm Jewish'* to anyone who would listen I was terrified that if I ran into an actual Jew I would be outed as the fraud that I was. I wasn't trying to deceive people for some twisted enjoyment. I just got my steps backward. My struggle was personal, not religious. I honestly hadn't even gotten to the religious part yet. My goal was to prove that I *could too* make my own decisions and that this was important. I figured I'd get in all the details later. I also decided to be a witch for a while, and then a "Jewitch"[31] (we'll talk about that later…). To me, becoming Jewish was a personal choice and I strongly felt it should be respected. I of course was demanding respect from my friends, coworkers and family as well as complete strangers. It hadn't occurred to me that I needed permission from the actual Jewish community first. First rule of being Jewish is that you are only Jewish if other Jews say you are.[32]

It is unlike any other religion in that the sociological collective group-acceptance part is equally as important as the personal development and spiritual part. Once you convert you're in, well, for the most part. If an Orthodox Rabbi converts you then you are in. Well, it depends on the Rabbi and how other Rabbis view him…its complicated. But suffice it to say a personal announcement is not going to cut it. All Christians feel as though they have entered an exclusive group via their belief. It doesn't matter if you are in a five-generation line of pastors; you are not born a Christian. Jews do not evaluate Jewish belonging based on religious belief. The more Orthodox you get the more your religious *practice* matters in terms of your group belonging, but even the Atheist Jew is still a Jew.

You cannot cease to be a Jew either.

I can safely say I am no longer a Christian. Other Christians would agree with me. But once I convert I'm a Jew for life.[33] This basic fact creates an ethnicity that one cannot simply adopt so easily. There is a language, body language, social structure, social expectations, fluidity and subconscious messages that come with an ethnicity and you can only learn it by being it. Now, there is a certain controversial experience in terms of converting to Christianity. As far as I can tell one is still considered a Jew but one who has made a decision forever cutting them off from the Jewish community. Accepting Jesus as the Jewish messiah is grounds for immediate termination. (See: Fiddler on the Roof). Oddly this doesn't apply to all religious conversion or exploration. If one were to explore Buddhism for example many Jews would roll their eyes but would still consider the person to be a Jew.

Islam[34], polytheism and Christianity seem to be the breaking line between a Jew and an *other*. You will often hear people refer to Jews who convert to Christianity as "Christians." In a sense, they are cut off completely from the community. You can return, however, without a need for re-conversion though which leads me to believe you are always a Jew. This is a really strange grey area for Messianic Jews whom I personally call "Christians" since they believe in Jesus.

I mentioned a "Jewitch" before and this is more of a novelty than anything. Jewitches are just Wiccans who are either Jewish and adopt pagan or Wiccan belief systems or they are people who try to merge Judaism (usually Kabbalah[35]) with the vast array of pagan practices that exist on the internet. I have mentioned this before at Jewish gatherings and most Jews have just raised an eyebrow. The point here is that Judaism truly is a stand-alone all-inclusive self-packaged religion that cannot be partially incorporated or blended with other things so easily. Sure, you can find a great deal of overlap between Jewish mystical belief and other Eastern beliefs, but in the end the source is Torah and you realize that everything else is unnecessary.

It is impossible to become Jewish from reading books on your own (except mine of course; it's all here). Trust me I have tried. You must be with other Jews.

It's sort of a 'love the one you're with' mentality. If you live in a larger community you have a better selection, but for me it was the Reform Synagogue. Those were my local Jews and those were the ones I needed to be with. Jews living in a small town, it seems, have a very different idea of their role than Jews living in big cities. What I found was that inside the synagogue everyone was Jewish, outside the synagogue it wasn't anybody's business. To this day, I'm still the only one walking around with a kippah on. I don't think anyone is ashamed or anything, they just grew up in a place where diversity is a hiring video you watch during training for a new job. When I tried on tzitzit[36] for the first time, people at work asked me questions, strangers took pictures with phone cameras and Jews said, *"Why are you wearing that?!"*[37]

I have found that you also cannot exactly earn your way in either. It's not a talent competition. You can own a kippah in every color but if you're not a Jew, you're not a Jew. The only way in is to marry a Jew or convert and that is just for Reform Jews…I gave up on wiggling into the Orthodox community years ago. I have to admit that I get it now though. After assimilating into this group for a decade I can safely say I get very annoyed when I watch a pretend Jew strut around. Anytime I hear someone in close proximity is Jewish my radar flares and my suspicions settle in. I eye their movements carefully and I choose questions designed to ferret out imposters.

I report my findings to the other Jews later.

At every gathering, there will be some unknown person that causes whispers and side-ways glances and people are aflutter with the possibility of a scam. I suppose you know you're a part of a group when you can easily identify who is not part of that group.

To this day, I still get very nervous when I meet a *real* Jew because I know they can see right through me.[38] It's in little questions like, *"Oh, so where are you from?"* Translation: *"I know all the Jews here and I haven't seen you before."* And when I admit with a sigh that I am, in fact, converting, they usually say *"ahh"* look to the side, look down, turn their head nonchalantly and change the subject.

I do the same thing.

It's funny really. When I first meet someone who confesses to mere enthusiastic interest in being a Jew I say *"ahh"*, look to the side, then down and then smile and change the subject. I have no idea why it is so difficult and I think I'm not supposed to talk about it. But the truth is ethnicity is tough to understand until you are in it. Luckily for me a nice Jewish family adopted me and spending time with them, our Yiddish choir and other social activities, I just slowly learned how things are done. The truth is, though, I can convert with the best of them but I will always be trying to be Jewish.

It took me a long time to grasp why this suspicion existed. I grew up in a religious environment that encouraged stalking as a means to incorporate new people into the faith. Once you shook hands you were family and soon people would be calling you on prayer chains and for "fellowship" events. If you visited my church you just never left again. The idea of expressing interest – *at your very peril* – in a religion and to be little more than a mild curiosity baffled me. It also pissed me off.

I worked hard for this and no one seemed to get that. The fights I had with my family, the mocking of my friends and the near constant stress of trying to balance new and old identities was sometimes maddening. Every time I chose to wear my kippah I had to make a choice to keep it on and upset my grandmother or take it off and hide it away to maintain hostile peace. It was simply unspoken in my house. My father refused to acknowledge it.

I was Jewish at work and I was Jewish walking around in the mall, but at home I was just causing trouble. To think that this meant nothing was infuriating. I deconstructed an entire half of my life's worth of religious belief and instruction, built an entirely new social identity and even changed my name and the best I get is a *'oh that's nice dear'*?

There were several points along the way when I just wanted to give up completely. I felt that it was just too difficult to fight one world who wanted me to stay and one world who didn't seem all that interested in letting me in. Something inside, however, kept me going but I can honestly say that it was not always easy.

There was never really a *faith* to hold onto. No spiritual fulfillment that justified my journey, only a sure knowing that the end was worth the travel even if I didn't know what it was going to be like. I struggled to imagine a Jewish life any different than the one I had fabricated piece by piece myself. I felt that after 5 years, 6 years and more that to have my entire identity reduced to a simple ritual was almost insulting. How was dunking myself under water, repeating a few lines in Hebrew and having my willy symbolically stabbed[39] going to make me any more Jewish than I already was? I became fond of saying, *"This is as Jewish as I'm going to get."*

I liked my tattoos and I wanted more. I enjoyed liking guys and I wasn't planning to stop that. I would give up bacon but cheeseburgers? No way. There is a line.

I just didn't get it.

And then, over time, I gradually did.

4

Chanukah Oy Chanukah

Chanukah is possibly the single best example of what converting feels like. No other Jewish holiday allows you to fully appreciate the transition over the years into this new life. Chanukah is the single most important Jewish holiday of all.

*snicker

Ok, so I really thought that when I first decided I wanted to become Jewish. In fact, it was really the only holiday I was aware of. The High Holy Days[40] were vague, Passover[41] was just the other part of Easter and then there was the tree one that I didn't really understand, but Chanukah had a Rugrats special[42]! I started my journey in March and I celebrated my first Jewish holiday on...you guessed it: Chanukah.

I will always remember my first Chanukah. Oh, the joyous laughter, exchanging of gifts and happy songs in front of the fireplace. No, wait, that's Christmas. The first rule of becoming Jewish is that Chanukah is not the Jewish

Christmas. I remember a news anchor, whom to this day I scowl at whenever I see her in real life, saying: *"And tonight begins the first night of Chanukah, a holiday many Jewish people celebrate instead of Christmas."*

That first year I was hyper sensitive and had already spent months building up an indignant self-righteous queue of discrimination and oppression for my new religious choice in my head. When they started playing Christmas music in October that year I was livid. There were several store managers that had to hold onto a look of sympathetic concern as I ranted about their Christian oppression of minorities and such.

I actually tried to find a menorah at Wal-Mart but settled for 8 glass candle holders and 8 multicolored full-sized taper candles which I sat on my TV. Yes, you read that correctly. I purchased 8, you know, for 8 nights[43]. This is what happens when you only read books. I set it up when my dad left for the evening and I cautiously lit the first candle (on the wrong side) and gasped in utter awe and appreciation of the moment I had just experienced. Then I sat down and waited until I got bored and then I blew it out. I don't know what I was expecting to happen, but I was a little disappointed that nothing inspiring did. I continued this for 8 full days until I had a blazing line of fire sitting on top of my TV set. My dad just rolled his eyes and left the room.

The first thing he said to me when I told him I wanted to become Jewish was that I better not expect to get eight days of presents.

Chanukah at work was also interesting. Places of employment are always fascinating during the holidays as people balance how much religion they bring and how much glitter they intend to share with their coworkers. Some insist on full dress Santa-themed sweaters and hats while others keep Nativity scenes on greeting cards close to their desk. Some spend the entire two months ahead of the event protesting the other's anticipated decorations.

Counter to my expectation of hostility from my coworkers for daring to squeeze a menorah next to their beloved Christmas tree, my coworkers were always incredibly enthusiastic about Chanukah. They too only knew of its existence and ever since that Adam Sandler song[44] felt well versed in all of the traditions. Over the years people would eagerly ask me, *"When's Chanukah this year?"* and *"Are you going to light candles at work?"*

People love Chanukah.

I have found over the years that I tend to decorate for Chanukah in public largely for the enjoyment of my coworkers as decorating at home seems silly. I don't have children (well, a cat but have you tried to get a cat to wear a yarmulke?). My Jewish family holds a small celebration that I enjoy, but that wouldn't occur for several years.

Before the 1950's people lit candles, had a nice Shabbat dinner (on Shabbat) and they ate latkes. The biggest controversy and excitement was over who used apple sauce for their latkes and who used sour cream.[45] Then Frosty and Rudolph happened and people started going Christmas decoration nuts beginning in July. Naturally Jewish children cried out in unison *"Where is our Santa?!"* and the Chanukah Bush[46] was born.

I had a Chanukah Bush.

Look, Christmas trees are one of the single most awesome inventions of mankind and they are so pretty and I just really wanted one when I was like 23 and had my own apartment. My grandmother always had several Christmas trees, large and small, with decorations carefully selected and placed each year. One tree was exclusively for decorations from Christmases past which included ones I had made in pre-school as well as my father's and even some of her own from childhood. The others were themed every year and she spent absurd amounts of money and effort on them.

I grew up decorating these trees, and the yard, and every other available inch of space in her house with festive Christmas joy and they are some of my happiest memories. Conversion books always say that holidays like Christmas are the hardest to let go of for Jews-by-Choice and they are damn right! I loved my Christmas tree!

I continued, of course, decorating festive trees with my family while I lived with my dad and continued with my grandmother until she passed. But I dreamed of the day I would have my very own Christmas tree with decorations chosen by me. Yes, the whole 'I wanna be Jewish' thing got in the way but deep in my heart I knew I would have a Christmas tree of my very own one day. I worked in retail (including two stores devoted to house decorating) and had spent years helping other people select the perfect wreath or ceramic snowman set. I spent those same years constructing my tree in my head in anticipation. When I was 23 I finally got my wish!

If you haven't gotten the subplot of this yet, I lived at home until I was 23.

That first holiday season I decided that I was going to be the most multicultural open-minded holiday celebration master that ever lived. My dad's new wife had a Christmas tree that you put together branch by branch (with color-coded bent wire ends) and she was buying a new one so I took it home. I built it all the way to the top until just the tiny tree-shaped topper was left and I placed one of the back branches on top. Ta-da I had a Chanukah *Bush*.

Really, it looked like a bush. I thought this would cancel out the whole "Christmas" part and would make it Jewish. Really.

I had enthusiastically selected a series of breathtaking ice blue and velvet blue holiday bulbs with ice blue lights and several sizes of six-pointed star shaped crystal (well, plastic) snowflakes too! Very Jewish[47]. I constructed it carefully balancing the size and shape with the colors perfectly. When I turned it on I gasped in awe at my creation. The moment I had been hoping to realize was there and more amazing than I had imagined!

I also put up a menorah I bought online and I used the tree topper as a miniature Christmas tree with tiny ornaments and lights. I might have acknowledged Yule and Kwanza too I don't remember. For a solid month, I enjoyed my Chanukah Bush and I excitedly told everyone I knew about my creation. I became one of those dreaded people whom I will reference later that caused non-Jews to say *"Oh, I know a Jewish person who has a Christmas tree!"* I apologize, I was young. I didn't know.

That was my one and only Chanukah Bush however. Once I got it out of my system the following year I decided that despite the many Jewish-themed representations, a six-pointed snowflake is not a Star of David. A Christmas tree is a Christmas tree and there just isn't a way around it. Yes, they are pretty – so pretty – but they are not Jewish. With a heavy sigh, I settled for a Chanukah (with the actual word in it purchased on the internet) wreath. It had glitter and everything.

These days I don't do much more than set my Chanukah bear holding a dreidel[48] next to a menorah on my shelf. I thought about purchasing all of the wondrous Chanukah-themed house fixing's you can find but I always waited too long, had too little money or realized no one comes to my house for holiday stuff because I always go to theirs. Also, I have a cat. I lost many a good dreidel to my cat.

None of my close friends are religious so we have holiday parties on or around Christmas (once during Kwanza because it was easier) and I try to make them watch *The Hebrew Hammer*[49] as their Chanukah participation points for the year. They still give me "Christmas" presents although after a decade they now call them "Chanukah" presents. With my Jewish family, I do sometimes have a special dinner with them on the Shabbat during Chanukah and of course our synagogue has a special Chanukah dinner and lighting.

Truth be told if Chanukah happened at any other time of the year it would be significant to Jews who take our holidays and remembrances seriously and others who hold onto the more folk tradition aspects. I doubt we would have giant inflatable dreidels with arms and smiling faces. Chanukah is actually a very beautiful and meaningful minor holiday with a great story of Jewish heroics, bravery and cleverness. It has an actual miracle and the simple beauty of enjoying the Chanukah candle lights contrasts to the incredible story that inspired the lights themselves.

The fun and the silly decorations created in a frail attempt to mimic the overpowering Christmas experience reduce the true joy this small holiday. If you get caught up in trading out snowmen for "Chanukah dudes" (because it looks like they are wearing little yarmulkes and I love them) and Christmas wreaths for wreaths covered in dreidels you end up forgetting the quiet joy that comes from sitting as a family and watching the glow of the candle lights bounce around the walls. The story becomes less significant if Judah Maccabee[50] is little more than a comic book character.

Chanukah is not the Jewish Christmas (although Jesus is said to have celebrated the festival in the New Testament)[51] and it can be a lot of fun. But the important thing must be to remember that Jews for centuries lit menorahs and put them in their windows at their very peril and the miracle of Chanukah is more significant than just a little oil.

5

Political Jew

I am a Conservative Libertarian. I am also a Conservative/Reform Jew. Neither of these things are in any way connected. If you say, "Conservative Christian" you know exactly what you are getting. "Conservative Jew" however is vague. Let me explain. (Please note: All sentences below should end with the phrase: *"well that is not necessarily true..."* This will help prepare you if you decide to state this or anything as fact to an actual Jew.)

Judaism comes in many flavors and the larger branches are well known: Reform, Conservative, Orthodox, Chassidic, Reconstructionist. Each has a purpose and origin that make them as distinct as Christian denominations and below is my best take on the whole thing. Many Orthodox Jews will, of course, argue that there is only one Judaism and all of the titles are varying levels of observance. Chassidic Jews are Orthodox and Conservative Jews can be close to Orthodox (Conservadox) or close to Reform or really somewhere in the middle. Reform and Conservative battle each other over who is the most popular and numerous in the United States while Orthodox tend to sequester themselves in smaller groups and avoid such nonsense.

In the 19th Century Jewishness changed[52] (well, to be fair it never really had a default setting but for the modern period this works). If you refer to a "Polish Jew" to a Jewish person whose family lived in Poland you are likely to get an earful of how there was no such thing. Jews lived in Poland but they were not Polish. Jews were not given the same rights or recognition in other countries and were easily removed when the mood hit the larger population in previous eras. In the 19th century, however, this began to change in some places allowing Jews to better integrate into the larger society. Tragically a core of this experience happened in Germany.

German Jews found themselves able to live amongst gentiles openly and many took this opportunity to abandon all outward expressions of Judaism to better blend in. Yiddish[53] had long been the language of Jews across countries where Hebrew was the language of prayer. Now Jews were engaging with gentiles equally as they did with other Jews in public. In Germany, Jewish intellectuals decided that the strict lifestyle and religious practice of Judaism as they knew it (Orthodox) was constricting and the actual source of anti-Semitism from the outside. They envisioned a Judaism that brought history and a traditional viewpoint into a beloved focus but did away with the religious traditions they felt were too restricting.

For example, it was decided that the pursuit of reclaiming Israel as the land of the Jews should be abandoned and that Germany would become the new Zion. You can see how that turned out. Kosher rules were dissolved, Shabbat was moved to Sunday and Synagogues spoke mostly German and used organs during services. Circumcision was removed as were all outward displays of Jewish law (head coverings, Tzits, payos etc.). At the first Reform Rabbinic graduation they celebrated by eating as many non-kosher items as they could.[54]

Over the years, Reform Judaism dissolved all distinctions between male and female roles. Men and women sat together during services and women became rabbis. At the beginning of the 20th century in the United States the vast majority of synagogues were Reform.

Reform Judaism of this period seemed focused on taking the cultural and ethnographic aspects of Jewishness as their primary identity. They still had services but in some, Hebrew was completely absent. Jews could marry non-Jews with ease and men no longer wore yarmulkes. Synagogues resembled churches in practice and appearance. The organ music flowed out disguising the practice inside from those walking by.

Reform Judaism today is more a mixture of religious practice, spirituality and modern liberal/progressive thinking. Liberalism in the United States and Reform Judaism are often so close in ideology that it is difficult to separate them. (See: Social Justice[55]) While the hostile rejection of Jewish practice is not nearly as aggressive, Reform Judaism is often very fluid and grey on all matters of Jewish faith and practice. There is a Reform view that belief in G-d, the sacredness of Torah and the following of Jewish law are nonsense and should be removed completely. There is also a Reform view that one's personal level of observance should be respected and Jewishness can be a multitude of things ranging from an ethnicity to a strong religious practice. Something that is common is the idea that there is nothing one *should* do to be Jewish (except believe in Jesus. We all seem to agree you can't do that).

As you might have gathered, I am not a big fan of the "to hell with tradition" Reform Judaism although I am close with a Reform Rabbi. This rabbi takes the view that your personal observance and enjoyment of Judaism is all that matters and she takes on Judaism as an incredible act of personal development and knowledge. While I sometimes feel insecure by the open fluidity of her perspective on Jewish law and ideas I am grateful for her enthusiasm in supporting my personal level of Jewish practice.

I didn't always like Reform Judaism, though, for one primary reason and that is the above-mentioned origins. Reform Judaism was formed to completely rewrite the

Jewish practices that for centuries people had literally died trying to hold onto. Jewishness is not just a cultural identity. It is not just an ethnicity. Judaism is, I believe, a sacred and holy expression of G-d speaking to us in the best way He could so we could understand our purpose here. The prayers, the language, the laws are what held Jews together across centuries and vast, hostile countries. It is what kept alive a faith that hundreds of years have tried to snuff out. The oppression of Christianity in centuries past, the barbarism of Islam, the secular exterminations – all of it survived because of the sacredness held by Jewish people to their faith.

Judaism didn't need to be reformed, in many opinions, to be more like those who worked so hard to destroy our ancestors. When a Jew today rolls their eyes at saying a prayer or laughs at another Jew wearing Tzits many consider it an insult to the Jews who died desperately trying to preserve these practices for their children, knowing that a single generation could lose Judaism forever.

There is a parable that I feel illustrates this perspective:

> *A rabbi who lived a beautiful and mindful Torah-observant life died and upon standing in front of the gates to the great hall of learning he was stopped. The man shook his head denying him entrance stating:*

"I'm sorry Rabbi, but you cannot enter this hall of learning with the others. "

The rabbi, stunned responded. "But I lived a good life! I followed Torah and studied every day! I taught my children and the children of my congregation to love and respect Torah!"

"Yes", the man said, "But when you prayed over your challah every Shabbat you did not do so with a full heart. You lifted the bread in a casual way and muttered the words anticipating the meal rather than the prayer."

"For that I am denied?" The rabbi shouted back.

"Yes. But there is something you can do. If you return to Earth as the seed of a wheat and grow into a strong wheat that is used to make a challah and that challah is prayed for by a good Jew who prays with all of his heart you may return and be allowed into the great hall of learning."

The rabbi thought about it and agreed although he did not know how, as a mere seed, he would ever be able to accomplish such a task!

He became aware of himself underground and as the cool earth around began to warm he hoped and prayed that he would sprout and receive sun in a good part of the field where he would be harvested. As he grew he worried he would not be tall enough or bright enough to be noticed and may fall to the wayside. He grew taller and he was harvested but he worried he would be used for something other than flour. As he was ground into flour he worried he would never be used a bread and if he was certainly not for challah.

He worried and prayed and then realized by the heat of the fire he was being baked into bread. He prayed it would be challah. As he cooled on the shelf he gasped in amazement that he had made it this far and was indeed now a challah waiting to be purchased, but he worried he wouldn't be purchased by a Jew. Many Jewish customers came in that day and he worried that each would be a good Jew who would pray over him with a full heart. Finally, a man came and purchased him. Setting him down on a Shabbat table the rabbi was joyful and amazed he had gotten this far and was now on the prepared table of a good and observant Jew. He knew he was soon on his way to the great hall of learning! As he was lifted his anticipation grew and then...the man said nothing merely setting him back down and began to cut him into pieces.

Appearing back in front of the man at the gates the rabbi lowered his head in defeat saying:

"I did everything I could do in such a limited way. I prayed and hoped but how could I control the words that a man says? Who was this Jew who would buy a challah for a Shabbat dinner and not even pray over it?"

The man paused and then said: "That was your son."

The rabbi backed away in disbelief. "That is not possible! I raised him to love and honor Torah and Judaism! How could he do this!"

With a sad heart the man said: "It is true you raised him in the ways of Torah, but he watched you lift the challah and mutter out a prayer with no feeling all his life. Why should he think praying at all is necessary?"

If you can shrug off the little things and dismiss them as unnecessary, it is argued, then soon bigger and bigger things fall away too. If a boy doesn't need to wear a kippah then why will he wear one as a man? Will his son wear one at all? Why should his son choose to not eat pork or shrimp then? Why should he be Jewish at all?

It all depends on the Jewish leaders, families and the Rabbi how this turns out. My Reform rabbi is filled with insight, joy and enthusiasm for the depths Judaism has to offer. Her focus is not on enforcing observance in her flock but rather to inspire and awaken curiosity in them to explore their faith. I believe in the traditions, but I also appreciate the creativity that can flow from the Reform perspective as well.

Conservative Judaism was formed with the idea that Orthodox Judaism may not be able to survive in a modern world but Reform Judaism could dismantle Jewishness forever.[56] Jews felt they needed to conserve Jewish religious tradition while still adapting to modern life. Conservative Judaism believes that the Torah and Talmud are of divine origin. They respect and honor the rabbis and continue to question and evaluate life through the eyes of the Talmud and Torah. There is a great importance on maintaining Judaism for this generation so the next can prosper as well, rather than losing those who choose not to embrace Orthodoxy.

For me I feel that Torah and Talmud are divinely created and meant to be studied and followed. I do think there are things we must do because G-d said to do them. The joy of a mitzvah is the act of doing a mitzvah. Conservative Jews do believe that Jews must observe the commandments and that they cannot simply dismiss them.

Conservative Judaism does, however, allow women to be rabbis and accepts gays and lesbians openly. They still do not perform inter-faith marriages and they do feel that proper conversion requires circumcision and the mikvah ritual. The Mitzvot should be followed and Torah and Talmud study are vital. They observe the Sabbath and are Kosher.

Scientific exploration is acceptable and questioning the stories and timelines in the Torah is also acceptable. There isn't a literalism in their viewing of the historical events. G-d is real and honored and His experience is understood in the Talmud and Torah. Hebrew is used in services with much more frequency.

Politically, Conservative Jews can be more conservative than liberal but it is not as clear cut as Reform Judaism is. Conservative Judaism is very much focused on compromise. Conservative political beliefs are fairly solid and not prone to compromise (as are liberal beliefs) so it is fair to say you would likely see more moderate perspectives. It is, however, easier to be a Conservative Jew and a political conservative.

I deeply appreciate the centuries of observance in which Jews have lived since their origin at Mt. Sinai. While I know that I am not currently ready to embrace Jewish law to its fullest I respect the significance of it and understand that I am missing out on an experience few have had in the whole of humanity. To intentionally remove oneself from the depth of Jewish experience is to deny oneself the most unique human embrace of G-d the world has known.

Now, you might begin to realize if you go to a mixed shul that Conservative Judaism and Reform Judaism blend together a lot. It can be said that Reform Jews choose how observant they want to be and Conservative Jews know how observant they should be. Both take from each other and are truthfully becoming less distinct rather than more distinct.

Orthodox Judaism, (you know, formerly known as "Judaism")[57] is a newer term which is usually only useful for people who are not Orthodox. The Orthodox themselves just understand their practice as being Jewish. While there are many levels, layers and sects involved with Orthodox Judaism their basic understanding is that they are living Judaism as Judaism was meant to be lived. The Torah and Talmud are literally the word of G-d and while questioning what exactly G-d was talking about is a huge part of the religion, the idea that these two sources are somehow man-made is not acceptable.

That is the big difference between Conservative and Orthodox. Conservative Jews kind of say *"whoa, wait a minute"* and Orthodox Jews go full force. Orthodox Jews also tend to follow the idea that Jews must separate themselves from the rest of society in order to maintain solidarity and typically dress very distinctively. If you close your eyes and think of a Jew what you see is likely an Orthodox Jew.

Orthodox Jews truly understand that to be a Jew is to be responsible for a lifestyle that one cannot simply avoid if they don't like it. There is no lesser level of observance that is acceptable. Each Jew is responsible for themselves to maintain the highest level of Jewish observance. As a whole, Jewish observance directly impacts all Jews, but individually one must choose to be observant. Orthodox Jews don't see Judaism as a mere culture. They see Judaism as a powerful gift from G-d to light the world with His commandments. The reason they do not take in converts so easily is because making a Gentile a Jew can turn a good person into a sinner.

Jewish law is not up for debate on practice, only details of how one practices. *'Can you ride an elevator on Shabbat? Well as long as you don't push the button it's ok.'* Questioning how we observe the law is the primary focus rather than debating if we should observe it or not. Ironically Orthodox Judaism is a culture and ethnicity based on the idea that Jews congregate together to prevent each other from being pulled away. An entire world exists which is only faintly reflected in Conservative and Reform Judaism. Conservative Jews can fully integrate into their outer society while maintaining Jewish law privately. Orthodox Jews never cease to be Jewish.

There is also a Modern Orthodox who do not physically resemble the long beard and curly side-locks[58] one thinks of as an Orthodox Jew. Chassidic Jews are Orthodox but are distinct in their own way which I do not fully understand but can appreciate. There is also the concept of the "Ultra-Orthodox" which we hear about in Israel who sometimes border on extremism.

It's easy to state that Orthodox is correct or incorrect and one of the others is the best kind of Judaism. Unfortunately, there is a great deal of battle within our ranks over who truly represents what Judaism is. Orthodox may appear static and eternal but in truth it evolves just as dramatically as the rest of us. I do see a deeper place in Orthodox Judaism, but I also think Reform and Conservative Judaism offer ways to keep Jewish life alive and new.

When I first walked in the doors I was fascinated by the idea that gays were fully accepted into Jewish life. This was a huge selling point for me because being gay was such a spiritual issue when I was a Christian. I remember breathing a sigh of relief when I found out that my sexuality was simply not an issue. I liked Reform Judaism then because it did not impose restrictions onto my life. I felt I could build a Jewish life with whatever I chose to build with (and then we got a Chanukah Bush.)

Over time I moved sharply away from the Reform concept and embraced Orthodoxy as my compass. It wasn't until meeting my new rabbi that I began to see my focus simply went from one place to another without fully appreciating all that was in between. I hope to one day see a Judaism where Jews themselves simply refer to their religious experience as being "Jewish."

6

What Kind of Jew are You?

I am completely making this up but one day you will begin to notice Jews here and there and will think to yourself: *"Ha! He was right."*

I mentioned before that when I was a kid a "Jew" was pretty much a background player in an Easter play. Jews wore lots of robes and had beards and that was kind of it. I honestly do not have a memory of "this person is Jewish" until I first walked into a synagogue. Jewish to me really meant "Old Testament." I have found, over the years, that many people are disappointed in the lack of Jewishness Jews around them possess. Everyone has a mental picture in their head and most Jews never live up to it. The lack of grasping what a Jew is can be best understood by the many breathless outing of various Jewish celebrities that no one knew was Jewish.

Once you get past the Rabbi and/or Seinfeld[59] image of a Jew you start to see a world that goes farther than just black hats or rainbow kippahs. Part of becoming Jewish is literally *becoming* Jewish. You adopt an ethnicity which overrides your original. Adopting an ethnicity (or accessing the in-group) provides you with a certain appreciation of the subtler in-group categories. This is by no means comprehensive, but I can see most of the Jewish people I know falling into at least one of them.

Also, if any Jew who knows me reads this and goes *"hey…wait a minute…is he talking about me??"* the answer is *of course not. Don't be silly. Never.*

I Jew better than you

All groups have that class of person who believes they alone are doing it correctly. Judaism is unique in that in a lot of ways that person can actually be correct. There are standards of practice that can be followed to the letter and are approved by the most respected of Rabbis. But what most *I-Jews* have in common is that their view of Judaism is rarely observed by those around them. I know Jews who absolutely believe they alone keep "real" Kosher. When they say Kiddish they say it the right way and everyone else is doing it wrong!

I-Jews seem to understand their own Judaism exclusively by comparing themselves to other Jews around them. The fact that other Jews are not Jewish enough reinforces their own sense of Jewish self-esteem. This is not uncommon because outside of a tightly knit Orthodox community there are rarely standardized ways of handling the vast array of Jewish living. People living in smaller communities, for example, tend to do with what they can manage and over time cut a lot of corners. Also, Reform Judaism kind of defined itself by its rejection of Jewish practice and the resulting generations became less focused on Jewish tradition through daily practice.

I-Jews know their Judaism and no one is going to tell them differently. You may have read this or that on how to do something, but they know how it's really done. Any discussion will turn into why Jews are failing at Judaism as a whole. The subject of "those other Jews" comes up a lot.

This isn't a bad kind of Jew, it's just often the result of a lifetime spent in a community with people who don't appreciate or long for the kind of Jewish life that an *I-Jew* believes is possible. Also, this Jew can be very observant or not observant at all...the point is they are right.

I'm Jewish, I don't Jew

The polar opposite is the strangely obsessed Jew who openly rejects most, if not all, Jewish religious practice. Judaism has a flavor and a culture so deep and rich that many frolic playfully through it holding onto a unique identity that allows them access to a world others never see. Jewish art filled with colorful depictions of Jewish themes decorate their homes and they adorn themselves with Jewish symbols, speak in Jewish dialects and describe themselves as Jewish in every other sentence. They eat Jewish food and listen to Jewish music and they travel to Israel many times a year, but hand them a Torah portion and they roll their eyes and walk away.

An *I-Don't-Jew* seems to define their Jewish identity by the very fact that they ignore Jewish religious practice entirely. They mock observant Jews for not getting what Judaism is all about and get very bored with Jewish study and liturgy. They may even go to synagogue weekly but try to get them to talk about G-d and they'll change the subject. Liberal-minded, these Jews find the stuffy Orthodox lifestyle obtuse and old fashioned. They view it as sexist, homophobic and outdated. Judaism is free, colorful and vibrant! Why stay indoors studying all day? You should be living Judaism not studying about it!

Judaism is a culture for them and not really a religion. This is where someone can be both Atheist and Jewish.

To Jew or not to Jew?

Somewhere in the middle are Jews who feel very strongly that no side is right or wrong. Judaism is a spectrum of experience, observance and practice. All Judaism is equal and no one should say one is better than the other. Forget "real Judaism," it's all good. These Jews are open to any form of Jewish expression one can imagine from pure Orthodoxy to pure spirituality to just good cooking skills. This non-committal attitude allows a free-flowing movement of moderation and compromise between warring sides who firmly feel their Judaism should be the one that gets its way.

The good parts of this kind of Jew, a *Free-Jew,* especially for the potential convert, is that it allows one to explore freely without feeling pressure to assimilate without being prepared. I pictured my conversion as being very much like how I pictured Catholic school. I imagined a pile of dusty books and a grumpy old man with a ruler tightly held for quick slapping! A free-flowing Jew lets you set your own pace and find your own place in Judaism.

The negative part of a *Free-Jew* is that you never have any answers and can't find a solid place to balance on. Everything is answered with *'that depends'* or *'what do you think?'* and every statement is qualified with, *'well that's not necessarily true...'* There are few, if any, strong positions on anything. If you happen to enjoy structure this will drive you mad. Judaism is often characterized by its strict lifestyle. *Free-Jews* dissolve that with a smile and a hearty *'well there are lots of opinions'* response.

Because the Rabbi told me so

Some Jews are born Jews and they die Jews and they honestly cannot tell you why. They don't eat bacon because they are Jewish. They don't have a Christmas tree because they are Jewish. They go to shul on Friday nights because they are Jewish. It never really goes any farther than that though intellectually. If you ask them why they will shrug and say, *'Because I'm Jewish.'* Religious depth isn't something they avoid it just isn't something all that important. Ever watch *Fiddler on the Roof*?[60] Well there you go.

There is an underlining concept that one must practice Judaism even if they do not understand it because practicing and doing are more important than believing or grasping. You can understand how to be good at sports but unless you actually do it, well it's meaningless. So many Jews live Judaism exactly as they were taught by their parents and grandparents and don't question any of it. This can be both good and bad I suppose. For me it was always mildly annoying because I like to know and understand. To see people just shrug and go along seemed empty to me. But Judaism is a way of life and for lots of people it's their entire life, even if they don't exactly know why.

Happy Happy Jew Jew

Oy and then there are *Jew Jews*! *Jew Jews* are Jewish all of the time in the most obsessively brilliant way they can imagine.

They thoroughly enjoy the religious aspects of Judaism along with the fantastic Jewish experience, but only in the Sunday School sort of way. They love Jewish everything! You will find these in the form of older ladies who wear Star of David earrings, necklaces, bracelets and finger nail polish and celebrate every single festival and holiday like it's a Southern Christmas[61]. They bring food, decorations, songs and the biggest brightest smile you will ever see.

Also, they will know everything about you within the first 10 minutes of meeting.

This is a stereotype and it's absolutely accurate. I like *Jew Jews* because they make Judaism fun and they keep the kids entertained. You don't have the ideological conflicts you get with other cultural Jews when you want to enjoy the significance of a holiday and they always have cookies. Always.

Jewpression

The opposite of the *Jew Jew* is the *Sad Jew*. *Sad Jews* are sad all the time because they are Jewish and being Jewish means bad things happen to you. By now I am sure you are aware of the Holocaust, and the *Sad Jew* will be more than happy to walk you through it again. Remembering is a huge part of Judaism. Remembering the horrible things that have happened to Jews throughout history is vital to grasping the depth of Jewish experience. You and I will always lack the ability to truly understand the levels of history and generational memory that born-Jews inherit and that is a constant struggle for me, but I am fairly certain Jews weren't sad all of the time since Moses.

Sad Jews see the sorrow in the history they share with others and like to end stories with *'and then they died.'* This isn't just about big events like the Holocaust either, this is everything. Everything happens to them because they are Jewish and you need to know all of the details, and I do mean *all* of the details. No matter what the occasion there will be some horror that must be revisited.

The underlying theme here is that eventually bad things will happen to Jews again and if you plan on converting you need to be aware of this. Those of us who lived in fairly uneventful neighborhoods filled with average people just like us struggle to understand why others would actually hate us just for being part of a minority. While sometimes oppressively annoying, *Sad Jews* do often have a point. The world hasn't learned how to stop repeating history just yet.

Quiet, I'm Davening Jews

I like to call these *Real Jews*. *Real Jews* really *do* Judaism, like hardcore and every day. While many will cringe at the title, it's what I call them. They pray, they eat, and they sleep and dream Judaism in the most serious and Talmudic way possible. There is no exception for a dinner; they will not eat non-Kosher food. If it's Shabbat, you will just need to wait until Sunday, but not during morning prayers. They are like the strong beams holding up the tall and brightly lit building of Judaism even if they are rarely seen, because you know, they are praying.

Their Judaism is personal on a level I will never understand and sadly they will likely never show me. Unlike other observant Jews, these Jews find that their Jewish practice is just what is expected of them and they don't really need to explain why to you or anybody. Sure, they want you to observe like they do but it's none of their business. They pray and live quietly in groups but they never really let anyone in to watch.

EvanJewicals

The other kind of very observant Jew really, *really* wants you to join them in their journey of Jewish practice. *EvanJewicals* will go to the very ends of the Earth to get even the most hostile and annoyed Jew to perform even the smallest mitzvah. Think Chabad[62]. These Jews are like mythical fairies casting dust onto flowers to make them bloom and of course by dust I mean food. They give people food and try to get them to perform a mitzvah.

Evanjewicals, unlike their not-so-cleverly named Christian counterparts, do not seek out converts. You could have a single Jewish great-grandmother on your mother's side and they will hunt you down to light even one Chanukah candle, but ask them about converting and they will avoid eye contact. Judaism for them is a quest to bring all Jews back to Torah and live in a world where Jews not only observe but appreciate and build a future for Jews to always observe.

Wait? You're Jewish?

Some Jews are happiest when their Judaism is neatly packed away with other bits of their childhood they'd rather forget. I call them *Anti-Jews*. As odd as it may sound, there is a population of Jews you may only see on Yom Kippur in the synagogue. You may find out they are Jewish by whispers here and there but do not approach them on the subject! Hostility is often accompanied by the discussion of their Jewishness or lack of it.

Sometime after their Bar or Bat Mitzvah they wandered outside the synagogue, took off their yarmulke and never looked back. Well, except for Rosh Hashanah and Yom Kippur of course. Somehow, they have a complete and utter rejection of Jewish identity to the point of angry bitter avoidance, but Yom Kippur still holds them.

I'd advise that any Jewish person who avoids the topic is best to be avoided in said topic until you get a bit less of a *Joob*[63].

Formerly known as "Jew"

So, it is sad, but many Jews do find themselves abandoning Judaism entirely except for an identity and a wistful remembrance of their earlier life. You and I changed our religion, right? Why can't a Jew? Well technically they can't which is kind of their point in a way. You will find people who openly identify as Jewish only to simultaneously demonstrate Christianity or Buddhism. They are polite about your Judaism and they will talk about their Jewish histories with you, but they don't Jew anymore.

Usually there is no hostility which is nice and they also do not typically attempt to sway you to their side either. In fact, their Jewish past feels almost like a soft sad longing they just feel too disconnected from to recapture. They married a Christian and were maybe not very observant themselves to begin with and just adopted Christian practices. Perhaps they fell in love and legitimately converted to a new religion. Sometimes they just felt distant from what they hoped Judaism could be and found that depth in a different place.

I remember meeting my first *Former Jew* and there was sadness because I was so enthusiastic about my desire to become Jewish that it puzzled me that they would abandon theirs. But just as you do not want your parents to endlessly guilt you into coming "home" to your birth religion, it's not nice to badger them either. This is controversial, however, because like *EvanJewicals* practice, getting a Jew to perform even a single mitzvah is a great blessing.[64]

Activist Jew

Some Jews find their Jewishness in devoting every second of their life to completely non-Jewish causes. Many Jews interpret "mitzvah" as "good deed" and therefore categorize recycling as a mitzvah. Throughout modern history there have been Jews who chose to express their own sense of oppression by alleviating the oppression (perceived or otherwise) of other groups. The Civil Rights movement, Marxism, Feminism, interfaith dialogue – all of it was done by Jews who find fulfillment in saving others. This, naturally, has very good outcomes as can be seen in the Civil Rights Movement, but can also find itself expressed as "Social Justice."

Social Justice is a phrase conservatives will cringe at, similar to "Socialism" and liberals view as both positive and necessary. I am a conservative so I do my fair share of eye-rolling at the concept, however depending on your personal persuasion you may find this fits exactly into how you live your life. If you look at just about any major social movement you will find Jewish voices loudly marching forward.

Activist Jews are opinionated, loud and forceful in their view points. They often speak for "all Jews" and are often described as evidence that 'Jews feel this way' on any given topic. Typically, this finds itself more socially and politically focused but it is often founded in religious belief. Many Reform Jews feel strongly that Social Justice and activism are mandates directly from Jewish religious teachings.

Only Jew in the village

I was an *Only Jew* once, and I still am in some ways. *Only Jews* tend to be focused on the fascinating fact that they are the only Jew around in any given social situation. Often obsessed with minority issues like discrimination or diversity, *Only Jews* like to make it a point that everyone knows a Jew is in the room. Think of them as the anti-*Anti-Jew*. They use the word continuously, insist on kosher food options in the vending machine and demand company-wide recognition of Jewish holidays. You just try and tell them they have to work on Chanukah. Just try.

Jews like this find identity in the fact that they alone hold it and are usually very territorial towards other Jews. Being the only Jew makes them special. It's a common *Joob* condition and most outgrow it but sometimes born-Jews will embody this role and never ever leave it. One can have great Jewish knowledge or may have just read a funny Jewish calendar once several years ago but if one is an *Only Jew* one will be the singular authority on all things Jewish. Other Jews threaten their reign over the naïve and ignorant Gentiles who look to them for guidance on this very special link in the chain of diversity. Not only will you hear great tales of bringing 'the first' Jewish something to wherever they may be or even better being 'the first' Jew to hold a position, but you will also hear of the endless subtle anti-Jewish experiences one can only imagine in a workplace filled with people who love bacon.

I'm just saying, if you start a new job and you see someone whom everyone refers to as 'the Jewish one' in an affectionate way – watch out.

Faux Jew

Faux Jews, like faux fur, seem to be more and more common. They are a curious breed of individuals with questionable parentage who boast of being Jewish but never actually demonstrate it in public. Sometimes a *Faux Jew* is the *Only Jew* in the area and they are easy to smoke out. Unfortunately, you have no clue you are dealing with one until you have already forever connected yourself in brother/sisterhood with them in a public setting. If people love a Jew they damn sure love two Jews.

I have worked with a few of these individuals and I found out they existed when non-Jews announced, with barely contained enthusiasm, that they know another Jew in the building! The meeting is always awkward with each sizing the other up. We are both thinking the same thing: *'Is he really Jewish?'* Because Jews come in so many forms and we have a public face to maintain, we typically remain polite, but the first shared Jewish memory or holiday will usually reveal who the imposter is. In my experience, they are usually complete and utter fakes (um, see a few chapters back...).

Pick and Choose Jew

You will find *Picky Jews* the most fascinating I imagine. They confused the absolute hell out of me when I started. I was once eating with one who spent a solid 30 minutes convincing me he was an *I-Jew* and going on about the lack of Jewishness in our community and then smiled openly as he shoved a piece of bacon wrapped around a hotdog into his mouth.

For some Jews, it's all about the things they find relevant and everything else is to be ignored. You might not realize this until it's too late but it is very rude to point out when a Jew is breaking a rule. Christians can call each other out with ease; Jews do not. At least non-Orthodox Jews anyways. For years, I have watched *Picky Jews* obsess over one part of Jewish practice demanding a near Rabbinic ruling on the matter and openly violating other parts without a second thought.

Over time I have come to realize that *Picky Jews* have a very solid concept of what Judaism means for them and they fully embrace what they embrace and the other stuff they have a very good reason for not doing. Sometimes that reason is that it's just silly and other times it is a statement. The point is that they are expressing their Jewish identity in the strongest way they can by demanding observance of some while openly rejecting others.

Revolutionary Jew

Every once in a while, a Jew steps out of the masses and reinvents Judaism in an exciting and powerful way. Some were called Prophets, others great rabbis. Today we have Jewish rap artists[65] and pop-singing Yeshiva groups[66].

Being Jewish is often a balancing act between the very mundane and the exceptional uniqueness that only Judaism provides. Sometimes that scale tips over. Finding exceptionalism in Judaism is thrilling because there are literally thousands of places, times, themes and perspectives to search through. Breaking out and taking Judaism to a new level can be viewed as frightening to those who fear the loss of tradition and frightening to those who don't want things to be 'too Jewish.' Come to think of it, standing out is usually just frightening.

When you look in from the outside you see this inventory of color, art, style, invention, literature and debates. You imagine this endless world of creation all around you. Then you walk in the building and realize that it's all ok because *other* Jews did it, not them…and don't get any ideas. Standing out as a Jew has a historical significance that threatened every Jew in the area regardless of their own personal choice in Jewish lifestyle. Jews like to keep to themselves and not draw attention to Judaism as a whole.

If the others don't know we are here they will leave us alone. There is a good and interesting sociological reason why so many performers, actors, singers, writers and comedians are Jewish. But sometimes a Jewish voice is heard above the rest and a new way of enjoying Judaism is discovered.

He/She Converted Jew

I'm sorry to tell you this but you will always be a *New-Jew*. I prefer the term *"Joob."* Everyone knows there is a basic understanding that once you convert you are to be considered as though you were born Jewish. This is like a Rabbinic ruling and is totally a thing. Abraham and Sarah were converts and hello! Ruth[67]? But for the rest of your natural life you will be referred to by some Jews as the 'He/She Converted' Jew. Some get fancy and call you a 'Jew-by-Choice' which frankly is our term and should only be used by us.

New Jew Power!

But seriously, I know people who have been Jewish for decades and people still refer to them as converts. Your friends and Jewish family will love you as a Jew but it's important to know that whatever above category you best find yourself in you will always hold this one closest to your heart.

7

Twalkin' Jewish

You cannot be Jewish until you have heard the phrase: *'Ask two Jews a question and you'll get three opinions'* and not giggle-snort to yourself with a knowing nod and smile. Jews argue. Jews have always argued. The Talmud can be described as the longest argument in history. No matter what you say you will always – always – hear the phrase: *"Not necessarily..."*

W.A.S. P's do not argue.

I grew up in a culture where you were free to disagree as long as you kept it to yourself. Whatever grandma or grandpa (or father or mother) said was final. You could smack down a 100-page research paper on why you are correct on a topic and it would be completely ignored if the highest person in the hierarchy (in my case my grandmother) disagreed. Not only was arguing pointless, it was rude. Choosing to be rude and talking back could get you banned from the dinner table until next Christmas and it was entirely possible that if the right level of escalation occurred you would never speak to that person again.

You might say that my perspective on conflict management was to avoid it.

And then I met Jews.

Unlike many other religions, Jews are ingrained to question authority, including G-d's. This was unthinkable to me on a level that is difficult to grasp. In many Christian faiths, the very idea of questioning G-d is itself a sin one cannot recover from. People permanently lose their faith over disputes coming down to individual verses in the Bible. Entirely new forms of Christianity have been formed because of differences in interpretation as to exactly how the end of the world will occur in a time line[68]. Arguing is scary when you know that if you are incorrect it could mean your eternal soul, let alone being removed from the birthday card list.

There is a large painting in a synagogue near me of four rabbis in what appears to be a heated debate involving near-fisticuffs. One rabbi is even putting his hands up in a gesture that can only be interpreted as *'No! You #$%&! Idiot!'*[69]

I was introduced to this culture in a dive-right-in sort of way. I was honestly completely unprepared for it. Over the years, I had been asked to join the Yiddish choir and being the shy and anti-social person that I am politely declined many times. Finally, I decided to be brave and I went. This experience was invaluable to my evolution as a Jew but the primary area of improvement came in my exposure to and practice in arguing. The very first practice session taught me everything I would ever need to know.

First of all, when you have a small Jewish community Jews of many flavors congregate together for joined events regardless of their affiliation. We had very conservative and very liberal people and many in between. Reform Jews, non-Jews, Conservadox and two pagans were also involved. Just deciding on the first song to sing seemed like a TV political pundit battle. If it wasn't the song it was how to sing the song, what Yiddish word meant what, how to pronounce this or that and of course, who was singing it the way it traditionally was sung.

I was frightened.

It wasn't until the dinner after that I got my real taste of what Jewish arguing was all about though. They always ate at the same place and as nerve-shattering as it was to eat dinner with a new group of people, the most disturbing part was how the conversation flowed from very happy and joyful discussion on promotions and birthdays to very heated and grandly gestured fights and then back again. I quickly learned that finishing a sentence was just not part of their communication style and if you dared to breathe in the middle of one the entire conversation could change. Topic after topic the mood shifted and often broke into multiple groups. Suddenly you would be speaking to just two people while the other three shouted at one another and then began laughing and playfully smiling.

Now I was the rebel in my family in terms of my willingness to push the envelope on unpopular topics and I regularly spoke out in classroom settings, but even this was beyond my comfort level. I honestly didn't know how they stayed friends afterwards and I certainly was not comfortable tossing myself out to the wolves on a first meeting. That was actually a mistake because my awkward and uncomfortable quiet just caused them to notice me more and direct questions and answers at me. *'I can't imagine how anyone could think that! CHAD, you don't think that do you? Tell me what you think. You think I am correct. See CHAD thinks I'm correct!'*

No topic was safe either. Everything could turn into a heated debate and then fall comfortably into hugs and well-wishes while dividing up the checks. This is all normal, I soon learned, as I spent more time in Jewish social groups. Jews just like to argue. It's not that they like to upset people; it's just that there is no reason to get upset, especially when you're obviously wrong on the topic.

The rhythm took some getting used to as well. There are two kinds of classroom discussions, one where you raise your hand and wait to be called on and one where you shout until you are heard. I typically spoke in small groups by waiting for the appropriate moment to begin speaking where it was expected that everyone would make eye contact and politely wait for you to be finished before adding their piece. What I experienced was one person beginning a statement and then some keyword or concept triggering outrage in someone else regardless of the context of the not-yet-finished sentence and they would loudly interrupt to correct such an obvious mistake. Meanwhile two others who simultaneously disagreed that the out-of-context keyword or concept was incorrect in the first place jumped in to demand that the first interruption was uncalled for. The original speaker would still be attempting to go on with their sentence.

I learned that not only must you participate because awkward silence is the loudest thing you can do, but you must also dive in and not hold back punches. I struggle sometimes between politely disagreeing and expressing myself with boldness usually reserved for MMA fighting on TV. I found this to be just as difficult as not saying anything at all. You watch someone throw their hands into the air and shake their head in utter exasperation at the very idea you would say such a thing and then you respond with equal force and it's suddenly and unpredictably inappropriate. It was so confusing.

There is an art to this, like all fighting, where it is considered honorable to punch your opponent's lights out with an approved move but incredibly disgraceful to do so with a wooden chair. The same goes for arguing. I learned a new social skill in doing so and through many battles found that I could loudly disagree and eat dinner at their house the following weekend without a problem.

Not only is there very expressive arguing where a person can look you in the eye, call you an idiot and then invite you over for dinner, but there are *opinions* which is completely different. If you ate dinner at my grandmother's house and wanted to compliment her on a dish you would express wonderful enjoyment and say, *'Oh you must give me the recipe to this!'* knowing full well that its rude to actually ask someone for a recipe. Oddly it is also equally impolite to not ask for the recipe. My grandmother would then express enjoyment at the compliment, say thank you and respond by denying access to the recipe.

When you eat dinner at a Jewish person's house you are likely to hear that everything that could possibly be wrong with the food has occurred and there are many apologies for the horror you are about to experience. Things are too salty or not salty enough and nothing is fresh like it would be in New York from a kosher bakery and the host is very sorry for the disappointment. You would imagine that people would begin to overcompensate by expressing great enjoyment of the food, right? Nope. They will agree with the host and provide an endless list of ways to improve the recipe.

Unlike what I grew up with, Jews have no problem giving out their recipes and their own cooking advice on handling each recipe which will involve the most precise ingredients and measurements you will ever find. This is true on everything. I do not care what topic you think you have expertise on I promise you that in a group of Jews you will hear many ways of improving upon it. Everyone has an opinion, or several, and they are not shy to give them. Also, they never forget. If they told you to do something or gave you advice on something they will ask you about it later. You can't lie because they will follow up with others to confirm your story.

Moses himself could walk in and give a speech and every Jew in the room would shake their heads and express loud opposition to everything he said on any topic. The good thing about this is that it forces you to really be well equipped in facts and logic for any given topic you choose to provide your own opinion on.

Also, if you tell a story be prepared to be quizzed. You can declare yourself to have been an executive chef in New York, best friends with an astronaut and describe how you toured France all in the same year and W.A.S. P's will look to the side, then down, smile politely and change the subject. Often, they will nod with faux-impressed interest.

Not with Jews. They will ask you clarifying questions. They know someone in New York who ate at that restaurant you say you were an executive chef at who always sent their food back because no one can get salmon the perfect texture and she never mentioned you. You cannot bullshit your way through. They want details and they will remember. They always remember.

W.A.S.P's consider calling people out on their exaggerations or outright lies as unreasonably rude. You complain about them later with others when they are not in the room, because that's polite. Jews will tilt their head to the side, say *'no, I don't think that's true…'* and then pry out further details so they can better expose you for the fraud you are. It keeps you honest. They won't let you be vague. They will ask and if you don't answer they will call others over to ask you too. Some Jew in the area will be an expert on whatever you are talking about and they have no problem scoffing at your claims in public.

Also, you cannot idly complain. You can tell a W.A.S.P that you just got gang-mugged by police officers who danced on your broken and bloodied body and they will politely express something like *'Oh you poor dear!'* and then change the subject. You tell a Jew that you got poor service at a drive-thru restaurant when they forgot to give you a fork and they will call the manager in front of you and get you a coupon. Just try to vaguely mention feeling sick or having any mild social issue and they will immediately demand a full list of details and offer to call a doctor or psychologist or lawyer or whatever they think is wrong and will be half-way through dialing before you can politely ask them to please don't. Then they will follow up with you later.

Discussing anything serious is going to result in some action that will require follow up.

"Ouch!"

"What's wrong? You said 'ouch', is something wrong?"

"No, no I'm fine. Thank you."

"No. You look pale. Have you eaten? What's wrong?"

"Nothing, my head hurts a little. I have a sore tooth."

"Have you called a dentist? I know a dentist. You need that checked up on. It could get infected."

"No, no I'm fine. I will go see someone next week."

"No. I will call Doctor so and so. He took out my friend's tooth and he's wonderful and came to our fundraiser last year. He's Jewish. *dialing dentist at home *'Oh Simon Hello! Listen I need you to fit in a friend of mine…'"*

I once literally fell to the floor in agonizing pain from a tooth infection and could not afford a dentist and my grandmother, several of her friends and her pastor-brother asked if they could get me a glass of water and wished me well to get better soon. At Yiddish choir, I put my head in my hands for an unguarded 2.3 seconds and I had 8 people surrounding me demanding details of what was wrong. I left that evening with an appointment the following morning to a dentist. They followed up with me…and the dentist…and every once in a while one of them will still ask me how my tooth is doing. That was 5 years ago.

I learned that saying things like *'This stupid professor said…'* or *'I got a parking ticket and…'* had to be carefully done and with commitment because someone in the group would call the president of the college or the mayor and probably in real time. Jews just take care of each other. Something I had to change in my thinking was that idle complaining is taken seriously to Jews when it is often dismissed by non-Jews. I don't know why I'll be honest; it's just a truth that you cannot avoid. Jews care and take action, whether you want them to or not.

8

Jewish Family

I have a regular family and a Jewish family. I am lucky that I was adopted (as an adult) and they have been endlessly patient in my ongoing conversion drama. Shabbat dinners taught me more than any book ever could. Yiddish choir was the greatest gift to my development as I never would have interacted with Jews otherwise. I am on the board of a Jewish charity and coordinated the Jewish group for my college for years. I build and manage the websites for all the Jewish groups in my area.

I am not a social person. I'm weird, in case you have forgotten the first part of this book, and I have always had a small group of people who knew I existed. I really started this thinking I could just become Jewish on my own to fulfill some internal desire and be done with it. I didn't realize I would be required to actually join a people. Joining a people requires, you know, hanging out with them on occasion. This has been one of the toughest parts for me. I do not engage in groups that well. I am great when I get there and begin engaging, it's just getting me to go that's the hard part.

I spent my teenage years going home from school and spending the evenings by myself with my computer and TV shows. I have grown accustomed to my quiet 'me' time. Having people call me, email me and ask about my daily life is not something I expected. Up until the Yiddish choir I had few group experiences with Jewish people. I would go to services here and there but I always felt like a painfully obvious outsider just watching. I was too nervous to go to more intimate gatherings on Saturday morning or Sunday morning partly because I was always afraid of being called out for being a fake Jew and because no one was younger than 50.

Yiddish choir is exactly what it sounds like, you sing Yiddish songs in, well, Yiddish. Yiddish is unique because it developed as a language Jews could speak to each other over great distances. If you lived in France and another Jew lived in Poland you could communicate through Yiddish. Yiddish sounds exactly like German to me and they have similar origins. There is endless horrific irony in the reality that Germany was such a powerful part of Jewish experience before, well, *you know.* Yiddish requires both a mastery of guttural pronunciation and reading Hebrew letters although our songbook did primarily have everything phonetically written out. I just sort of learned everything through repeated singing and soon words began to make sense. Yiddish music is this strange mixture of incredibly depressing themes and beautifully uplifting musical rhythm. Singing the songs feels soulful even though the words themselves are not always so happy. People grow old, lose their belongings, get killed and generally suffer in Yiddish songs. They speak to the reality Jewish people lived through in so many places a times. When you sing a Yiddish song, you connect to the people who truly felt those words.

Yiddish songs also have the interesting reputation of being something Jews from many walks of life all find a connection with. Jews who are older often remember their parents speaking in Yiddish and the songs were often what they heard as children in the same way I heard *Mary Had a Little Lamb*. Being as I do not have Jewish childhood memories it was hard for me to connect to the music in the same way. Simultaneously though I now consider these songs to be my first Jewish memories. They were the first things I did with other Jews who became my Jewish family. Singing, learning and talking about these songs is what built my Jewish identity beyond the simple '*I am Jewish*' mental tape I created for myself.

I struggled very much with my own family through this process. When I first told my grandmother, I was 20, and she literally burst out in laughter. I think it was possibly the absolutely last thing she ever expected me to say and couldn't help herself. My father sulked away and refused to acknowledge it afterwards. Over the years, they slowly would mention my "beanie" as my grandmother called my kippah and while they never embraced the idea they never forcefully banned me either. I already told them about the gay, this couldn't be much worse.

As I have mentioned, my grandmother's brother was a pastor and so was her sister. Her father and grandfather were also pastors. My dad went to a Bible college but it didn't fit him and so I was the last chance to keep the heritage going. My great-grandmother reportedly held me in her arms when I was born and foretold my future as a great pastor like her grandfather.

As a young adult, my family relationships were so strained that I considered myself to be just a connection by blood to them and nothing else. My grandmother so very much wanted me to be a good Christian man married to a nice blue-eyed blonde-haired woman and celebrating our first child by the time I was really serious about this Jewish thing.

I think she saw it as rebellion and my dad saw it as another phase. It's not their fault either. I was a phase-happy young fella. I changed my life-plan as often as I changed my hair color which was sometimes weekly. But I have to say that never getting to share this part of my life with them is something I regret. A week before my grandmother fell very ill and shortly before she died from that illness she expressed interest in seeing my synagogue but she never got the chance. My dad died a few years earlier and he and I never once discussed my Jewish life choice beyond that first coming out experience.

Converts are encouraged to keep strong ties with their family and some rabbis won't convert someone who feels they must abandon their family entirely. The commandment to honor your mother and your father still applies. I never got the hang of integrating my family into my choice to become Jewish. Instead I just kept it to myself until there was no one left to embarrass and I allowed myself to be adopted by the Jews already in my life.

In my more recent connections to my mother, sister and their side of the family my Jewish identity is awkward, but not unwelcome. Although they try to ask about kosher food or Chanukah presents, I tend to be fairly low-key with them. My nephew and niece are autistic and I am not sure how well it would integrate into their worldview. Some of their family is very Christian as well. My sister did send me a picture of my nephew with a bowl on his head a few weeks after first meeting me however.

Sometimes the disconnect is internal, rather than sourced from your family. I choose to keep my Jewishness separate; they do not make it necessary.

I honestly do not know how other converts do this, especially if their family is strongly religious, but I think if I hadn't tried to hide it so terribly it would have been easier. I'm sure my sneaking around and refusing to answer questions to avoid the topic didn't help remove the mystique around the decision they already disapproved of. Of the things I would do differently if given the chance would be to experience Judaism with my family more openly. There were times when they expressed some sparkle of curiosity and I always brushed it away. I always thought that the less they knew the easier it would be for me; otherwise they might get too involved and ruin everything.

I tried hard to make a very clear distinction between my *before* life and my *new* life. I should have, instead, blended the two together.

Adopting my Jewish family was an exercise in trust. I was growing up all over again. I found myself in achingly polite and awkward situations, warm and loving moments, frightening crisis and true togetherness in the face of an enemy. I was accepted for who I was and who I was trying so hard to become with just the right amount of parental push to make better decisions. In many ways, even though this all happened in my mid-20's and is still ongoing, I feel this is the family I longed for when I was a child. I have friends who sometimes feel like parents, people I can share my feelings with openly and who give me advice and who expect me to do the same back. I have siblings whom I argue with and aunts and uncles I love to visit but in just the right amount of moderation. There are elders and children and it's all connected because we are Jewish. I got my Jewishness from the people who chose to love me when they had no reason to.

I never understood the Holocaust. The Shoah[70], as Jews prefer to call it really, had little more emotional effect on me than watching any other story of tragedy befalling a people. I would go to the Holocaust remembrance events and listen to them read names and sing the songs. I would watch the movies and listen to the speakers and flip through the books but I just didn't get it. Nothing ever resonated with me.

Some Jewish converts who also embrace reincarnation claim to strongly believe they died in the Holocaust in their last life. I just am not one of them. For me it felt like the Civil War. I could appreciate the horror, but I didn't feel it. I think, for me, this speaks volumes about the disconnection between my Jewish self-concept and Judaism in real life. I felt insulted that Jews didn't appreciate my struggle to be one of them, but I never considered that I just was not one of them.

My family did not die in the Holocaust. My grandparents did not lose their families only to flee to a new world to create a new life in a hostile land. I do not have generations of experience behind me telling the story of the struggle to survive with a life guided by Torah.

You cannot live in two worlds. Being Jewish is not a hobby one can start and stop as time allows. For born Jews it seems as though they compartmentalize everything and that appears to be what you are supposed to mimic but the reality is that it is always with them. For a convert, it is a struggle to let go of your former life so completely that you end up adapting the other world to your new Jewish life rather than the other way around.

That's why Orthodox Jews are so tough on converts. It's why they push back. From a religious point of view a Gentile has far less responsibility to G-d than a Jew does. To take a Gentile and make him a Jew without proper understanding of the responsibility is to create a sinner. Once you are a Jew you are a Jew with thousands of years of history and moral obligation placed on your shoulders. You cannot simply step away when it gets too heavy. But culturally as well, stepping into this role means abandoning your entire history in such a profound way that there are few other life experiences like it. As much as you try to blend your Gentile life in with your new Jewish life, the reality is that once you take this journey there are no other roads. You can't just put up a Christmas tree next to your Menorah.

Your life ceases to be your own. You become part of a history larger than anything you were part of before and even though you stand along the edge you still support the whole. Your actions speak for all Jews. Your works speak for all Jews. Your future will one day be part of Jewish history. If they come for the Jews again, they come for you too.

9

My Cats Are Not Jewish

I have three cats, six frogs, two crabs, several fish and a multitude of snails. None of them are Jewish. For some reason, Jewish people seem determined to make their various animals Jewish and you will occasionally see some horribly unhappy cat with a kippah strapped to his head on Chanukah cards. My cats do have Jewish names however, well two of them do, Morticae, Moshe and Freddie[71]. I freely admit that tried to make my cats Jewish. Early on I focused very much on forcing everything in my life to be Jewish. I got Freddie, which was my grandfather's name and then I got my other two and I felt it was very advanced and witty to name them authentically Jewishly spelled names. It helped build my story that I was-too Jewish. If people asked I would proudly announce my boys as, *"Freddie, Morticae and Moshe"* and the goys swooned. Jews either raised an eyebrow or didn't react at all because, you know, their animals also had Jewish names.

The Judaification of my life happened like this: I decorated my house with authentic Jewish artifacts, filled my bookshelves with authentic Jewish books, named my cats Jewish names, changed my own name to a Jewish name and then changed my appearance to look, sound and move Jewishly.

I changed my name?

Changing your name is not something converts do. Yes, you get a Hebrew name but that's not a legally binding thing, it's for calling you up to Torah. If your last name is O'reilly then O'reilly becomes a Jewish name. Most converts that aren't doing so to get married just keep their name. I had to be different.

My family name does legitimately have some negative connotations to it in the world of, well, KKK membership and we will leave it at that. If I were to have children I would not want them to be Jewish with that name. I changed my name because it was the final break from my old life. It doesn't take deep psychological insight to figure out why that is important, but to be clear every Jew who learns this about me thinks it's weird. Don't do it.

The decision to change my name came along after my grandmother died; exactly one month after if you must know. I had considered the idea for a while though because I was obsessed with this idea that to become fully Jewish I would need to abandon all aspects of my formerly non-Jewish life, otherwise it was just going to muddy things up.

No one told me I am not a Grim Reaper from *Dead Like Me*[72] and that its still ok to talk to my family. Well the rabbis are pretty clear about that, but I felt like it was an issue.

After my grandmother died I filed the very expensive paperwork to petition my name change, picked it out and then went to court to get it approved. The judge literally said *"Here you go; you have a new name, good luck with your life. NEXT!"* I was completely alone during the process and when I left the courthouse with my fancy new name it was entirely my own transformation. I had no family to explain it to and no one to second guess me and my friends were ambivalent. I did not talk to a rabbi first.

Becoming Chad Felix Greene (I'll give you a hint, my first name stayed the same) was a life-changing event in that I got the chance to redefine my entire life as I saw fit. As is typical of grandiose 20-something life-changing decisions, it did little more than just confuse everyone and it did not make me Jewish.

Where did I get Felix and Greene from? Well remember my little past-life regression? Guess what my name was then? Not Felix. I was Jacob Greene. Felix was because I wanted to use the first letter of my grandfather's name (Jewish tradition) and I liked the name. Chad Freddie Greene didn't work. In terms of my future book writing adventures it was an excellent choice if I do say so myself but regardless of my intention it did not make me a legitimate Jew. In fact, to this day Jews shrug it off as eccentricity and are not moved by the gesture one little bit. All three of my rabbis have titled their heads to the side like a confused dog and responded with *'...why did you do that again?'* My friends, by the way, still apparently find it weird but I cannot imagine myself without it now.

For me, changing my name was the ultimate solidification in my mind that this was real. I was dedicating my life to this and my life as I knew it was going to be Jewish forever. Also, I get to forever say *"my name is Chad Greene with an 'e.'"*

What about my Jewish name? That turned out to be a significant experience that I had not anticipated. I always assumed I would just take the name Jacob (Yakov). For some reason the Hebrew name thing did not have an emotional significance to it. I already changed my legal name so doing it again seemed unnecessary.

Having a Hebrew name is, however, a requirement for all Jews. I am still a bit fuzzy on the purpose as some Jews go by their Hebrew name all the time and others only use it for specific religious events. Two weeks before my conversion when finalizing the details my rabbi brought up the name topic and I suddenly realized that I had nothing to really hold onto. Taking Jacob no longer felt important. In so many ways my original goal of continuing my former life as Jacob Greene got lost in the details of my actual Jewish life.

Somehow Chad Greene became my Jewish identify and I built my Jewish life through my own actions and decisions. I wasn't fulfilling some larger metaphysical redemption; I was living this life exactly as I wanted. I was preparing to be Jewish for the rest of this life, not to complete the last one.

Being Chad Greene was all about building a life by my own choices and not pre-determined by my situation. I had struggled for this and now it no longer made sense to honor a past that no longer felt relevant to me. I decided this was one thing I could not decide for myself. So, I asked my Jewish family to name me.

It is unusual to do this. Most converts choose their own Hebrew name and it always has some significance to them. They find inspiration from Torah or other historical Jewish people or they choose to honor someone in their life or their own history. The Rebbe[73] would just tell people to choose the Hebrew version of their given name. Because of my history and because of my relationship with my Jewish family, we decided to do the same.

I became Shai Ben Avraham.

Converts typically take "Ben Avraham" or "Ben Sarah" and sometimes they take both. This is like "son/daughter of." We don't really think in these terms in our own world but from Jewish history this is significant. Since Abraham and Sarah were the first Jews and the first converts it makes sense. "Shai" is pronounced like *shy*.

When you try to find a Hebrew version of your own name its easier if your English name is a Hebrew name like David or Rachel, "Chad" doesn't exactly translate well. We went through many "ch" and "sh" sounding names but something about Shai seemed to fit. It means Gift in Hebrew. I thought that was meaningful to be named such a thing from my Jewish family.

One by one I have found significance in the Jewish artifacts around me. The Mezuzah, for example, is not to show the world you are Jewish as I previously thought. The Star of David is not meant to show your devotion to Judaism or to protect you from anything (which I never believed but I have heard.) I have worn a Tallit before in synagogue but it felt weird because it added to that feeling of being fake. Tzizt are wonderful if you get the right size, don't mind the square-shaped wrinkles that show no matter what and can figure out how to properly wash and dry them without destroying the fringes.

Jewish books like *Jewish Literacy* by Rabbi Joseph Telushikin and the *Artiscroll Siddur* are great to have around for referencing and it seems that every Jew has the same set of Jewish books for this purpose. It seems that with all of this there is no final completion. Everyone is trying to work into their lives these objects using the same standard books to make sure they understand what they are doing. My purpose in the beginning was in the 'I get to do it' theme and then slowly moved to maintenance because now that people saw I did Jewish stuff I needed to keep doing Jewish stuff and then I began to understand their significance and I wanted to do it right and now I feel that I am starting all over again.

Each time I walk past my mezuzah I pause for a moment and I think *'am I really doing this?'* I forget sometimes, often actually, that I am supposed to pause and remember to keep the commandments with me all day until I return home again. But too often I am leaving quickly and entering filled with thoughts and bags of groceries and I forget it. When I pause, I remember that I need Judaism in my life and this small symbol is the key to my devotion inside my house and outside.

I used to wear my kippah almost in protest to those who would say I could not. I remember my rabbi out in public at this anti-hate group solidarity protest thing everyone in town was involved in and I was wearing my kippah on purpose and he saw me, looked around, and then pulled out his own and put it on. I thought *'Ha! See, I knew I should wear this to show people Jews were here!'* I would wear it in public just waiting for someone to give me a dirty look or say something that would give me a feeling of standing up for my faith. I so desperately wanted to prove myself and in order to do so I needed something to stand up against!

As the years passed wearing my kippah became less and less of a statement and more of a personal commitment to this idea that I was going to live a life that required true commitment. I would put it on and look in the mirror and think about how significant it was in my life to do this. My faith was not inside my own head but was open for everyone to see and to criticize – literally on top of my head. I felt a personal responsibility to be a good person and hope people would see a good Jew. Then that became routine too. I put my kippah on every day before leaving my house and took it off when I came back home. It became part of my daily 'grab the wallet, keys and kippah.' I forgot I was wearing it and when people asked me what was sitting on top of my head I would squint and then remember. For more on this topic please see my children's book *What's That Thing on Your Head*?[74]

I forget. I wear this little hat because it's supposed to remind me of my commitment just like my mezuzah. I have spent so long trying to convince everyone else and myself that I am serious about this Jewish thing that I overlook the simple promise to G-d that I give when I exercise these practices. Wearing my kippah is not for others and it's not even really for other Jews. It's for myself to show G-d I mean it when I say I will obey him.

All the Jewish themed books, artwork and symbols in my home do not make it a Jewish home. I can wear a kippah of every color, tzizts, a Star of David necklace and hell I could grow a beard and curly sideburns and it doesn't make me Jewish. A hundred Israel flags and stars covering every square inch of my car, cubicle and front porch does not make me Jewish. Giving my cats Jewish names and tying kippahs to their heads doesn't make them Jewish either.

On this topic: why don't I have a beard? When I first decided to become Jewish I loathed the idea of having to grow a beard and I'm sorry, I really am, but curly sideburns just look silly. I respect Orthodox Jews and I get why they do it, I do, but it looks silly. The simple answer is because I don't want to have a beard and technically I am following the mitzvot because I do not shave with a blade the corners of my face or cut my sideburns to the point that the tip cannot be bent to touch the root. It's all about the technicalities sometimes.

10

Pimp My Judaism

The most tangible quality of human arrogance is the belief that we can determine, precisely, what G-d is thinking. Molding a religion to one's personal comforts is the second most tangible quality. I will admit my ignorance on the full picture of Jewish history and I will provide for the extent of this discussion that Judaism has always adapted to fit the needs of Jewish people over time. Ok cool. But the basic premise that I can walk into a religion and start tearing down walls and picking out color schemes is flawed. Judaism for me is a lifestyle. I feel strongly that Judaism has survived because of Jews' willingness to hold onto it no matter what the cost.

That being said, I walked into this process feeling that it was perfectly reasonable for me to create my very own Judaism and no one would mind. We have discussed the Chanukah Bush and I'd like to move past that please, but it goes so much deeper than that. I saw so much in Judaism that I was intrigued by but I also saw so much I did not understand, appreciate or approve of. I figured that since I was choosing to become Jewish it was only fair that Judaism accept me on my own terms.

Yeah, that didn't work.

Reform Judaism has no problem with this so I could have been a Reform Jew and for a while that is exactly what I was. Being gay, getting tattoos and even eating shrimp and clams seemed like a perfectly reasonable balance to the whole giving up Jesus thing. I looked to Judaism and I said *'What can you do for me?'*

I think I felt so distant early on because I didn't really get what it was I was doing. I expected Judaism to win me over. I wanted Judaism to surprise me, intrigue me and make me believe. Jesus turned stuff into wine and gold and shit, where is my Moses with his sticks that turn into snakes? But service after service I found myself completely and utterly empty. The pretty words felt hollow, the songs felt forced and the Torah felt like a museum piece.

I remember when I made the choice to believe. Belief was always something that happened to me when I witnessed something dramatic. One is made to believe. Choosing to believe is something utterly different. I felt there was something inside me that had to change in order to find Judaism because Judaism didn't need me. Judaism was happy just as she was.

I chose to accept the Torah exactly as it was. The Talmud was part of this belief and I chose to stop intellectually trying to understand it and to just try believing that it was the word of G-d. What if it is just as it is? How would I approach the commandments? How would I pray then? How would I view my life?

There are not many religious things that seem to go well when one believes the only motivation is 'cuz I said so' but Judaism is different. Judaism: *Just Do It* is pretty much the mindset of many Chassidic and Orthodox Jews. For a very long time I dismissed this as silly old-fashioned religious nonsense and associated it with all of the things I did not like about Christianity. I felt that blindly following rules was the worst possible way to find salvation in any form or situation. How can someone become enlightened if all they do is follow orders?

Judaism is unique in its premise. At Sinai, the Jews said they would do and *then* hear. They agreed to the Mitzvot before they heard what they were. This was a promise we made in accepting the Torah from G-d. Ever since we have devoted endless hours and pages to trying to better understand how to do that properly.

I like to imagine this whole thing like an old-fashioned watch. I can take the watch apart and look at all the pieces and say *'well, I don't know what this piece does so I'll toss it out.'* Eventually I'm going to have a very nice looking, but broken watch. In many cases taking just one piece out will ruin the functionality completely. What if the commandments are the mechanical parts to G-d's watch? What if he gave us the blueprint for how life works in the commandments?

So many of the commandments are strange and they do not make sense. Why can't I mix linen and cotton together? Why can't I eat shrimp? But when you imagine that it might be possible there is a bigger picture reason for all of it then it makes a little more sense as to why we should just do them. I do not know how G-d thinks and neither do the rabbis. They have the Torah and they have been trying to figure that out for centuries, but they do seem pretty confident in the notion that G-d wants us to do as He says. What if you saw all of the mitzvot as the gears to a watch? You could think of them as ingredients to a recipe as well. In either case, you know that each part makes the whole even if the part itself makes no sense.

Perhaps in the quest to help enlighten us G-d created a simple formula of daily actions that would create the end result of Jews being the light unto the nations. He did offer this to all the other nations first and we were the only ones who accepted. Ever since we have been tasked with building the stage for world peace. G-d put together this list of things and handed it over to us and basically just said *'Do these things and you'll see.'*

People often point out that Jews are different because we are free to question and challenge G-d. That is true, but I think people imagine this means that the arguments are over what we can and cannot do. In my experience, it seems the arguing is far more focused on what exactly following a mitzvah means. It is important that we follow the instructions exactly and sometimes they feel vague so we end up with elevators that stop on every floor in Israel on Shabbat so no one pushes a button and "works" or "lights a flame."

The sometimes-insane practices we see Orthodox Jews perform come from this obsession with making sure the commandments are followed exactly. Since we do not know G-d's thoughts we cannot predict how much wiggle room He provides on the rules He gave us. Orthodox Jews view this process as doing and then understanding. Do the mitzvot without question and then we will try to understand how to incorporate it into our ever-changing lives. This is viewed as adapting over the ages to make Judaism accessible but I feel it has more to do with trying to maintain this ongoing promise to our G-d who chose us because He believed we could do it.

I like to delve into the endless study of the commandments and even though I do not incorporate them like I want to, I believe there is value there. I don't think there is a magical completion moment when you successfully do all of them in a row, but I do think that keeping the mitzvot in your life on a daily basis makes you a better person. You make every moment important and significant. Every action you take, every piece of food you eat, every prayer you say is suddenly significant to not only your life but to the entire world of both Jews and non-Jews.

It is said that Moshiach[75] will come when every Jew either follows Shabbat perfectly or every Jew breaks Shabbat on the same day. I like knowing that my actions affect the entire world. I see nothing negative about believing this and I do not find comfort in controlling my faith to such a point that I decide which commandment is valid and which is not. For me they just have levels of accessibility, understanding and my own personal will to complete them.

This perspective sounds as though only Orthodox Judaism can be positive. Reform Jews are sometimes known to reject whatever doesn't fit in their current worldview. Some change the gender of G-d or include female references where only male references exist.[76] Others view observance to be beside the point and expression of Jewish community and unity is far more pleasing to G-d than the detailed minutia of day to day ritual.

In my experience, I have enjoyed the revamping nature of Reform Judaism in songs or expressions of prayer, but I also hesitate on issues where a mitzvah is in conflict and the attitude is 'meh, its fine.' But Jewish unity is so important that sometimes we can find compromise for its sake. During Sukkot[77] we shake the four species and the lulav. Part of the idea is that the four species of plants we shake represent different kinds of Jews with different levels of observance and knowledge. By binding them together we recognize the need to find a way to be together even with our varied differences.

For me the important thing is the respect given to Torah and the Mitzvot. I believe in the concept of 'do and then hear.' I feel there is deeper meaning. I want this to be respected. I don't believe we can just toss aside things we find pointless. But I also understand that we must find a way to bind ourselves together. Sometimes this means singing a traditional song differently to get enthusiasm and realizing that it still works because everyone is singing the prayer as they should.

11

Eating is the Hardest Thing I Do

I argue that eating is the single most difficult part of being Jewish. Kosher laws are the most complex and infuriating things you will encounter in this entire process. I can say that next to the Christmas tree issue, this has been the most destructive to my life that was. People think eating Kosher just means no more bacon but they honestly have no idea.[78] Interestingly this was one of those areas I thought about rebelling against early on. As mentioned, the first Rabbinic class of Reform Judaism chose to celebrate by eating every treif[79] item they could fit onto a plate as a show that the old ways were truly over. I tended to agree with them.

Eating ham was the first wagon moment in my new Jewish experience. I grew up in a family that wrapped ham in bacon and dipped it in cheese. We had ham all the time. Pork products were in just about everything I consumed. I was still living at home and so this made it particularly challenging when I announced that pork was no longer an acceptable food option for me. The response was something along the lines of 'then you'll starve.'

I really thought becoming Jewish would be easy in this way. Vegetarians do it all the time, how hard could it be? At first I decided that I was going to be 100% kosher and then I realized that even at my best I'd be lucky to get in 50% of the stuff I could actually buy from a store where I lived on that plan. I then decided that no pork would be good enough. You'd think giving up just one food option wouldn't be so hard but dear lord it was the toughest thing I had ever done. First of all I effectively banned myself from all of my favorite foods. I loved pepperoni pizza, ham, bacon, bacon with ham, bologna, hot dogs, spam and just about anything else you could fit a pig nose into that involved ketchup. I could sit and eat an entire package of bologna in a sitting and just love it.

Pizza was the first temptation. My father ordered pizza about four times a week and it was always a meat-lovers. Meat-lovers typically contain ham, bacon and sausage. As I watched my family gorge themselves on the tasty and wonderful meats I sighed with futile frustration at my new life choice which I had to keep up, otherwise people wouldn't take me seriously anymore. I figured that my meat-eating life had to change if I was going to prove this Jewish thing wasn't just a fad.

I was able to resist pork products despite my father's insistence on eating it at every meal for about a month before I broke down and had a pork chop. Oh, I missed pork chops. I can still taste it. My dad always made them extra crispy and as I chewed with total euphoria and disgust I knew that I had ruined everything. To be sure my father never did take my 'no-pork' thing seriously. He always just thought I was being stubborn. My grandmother was worse. She cooked dinner and you did not ask her for something that was not already on your plate.

She invited me over for dinner often and would put pork-something on my plate with a smile and a gleam in her eye that said, *'you're not getting away with this Jewish nonsense in my house.'* She loved to torture me with her wonderfully tasty and lovely pork-themed dinners and I would always surrender justifying it all as keeping the peace for my family. G-d liked peace, right? Mmm pork-chops.

But as the years passed I began to realize that most people directly associate a person's level of Jewish authenticity by what they eat. A Jew can pray every morning, have curly sideburns, a beard, wear a yarmulke and say *"oy"* with every breath but if they ate shrimp they were proof Jews just make the whole thing up. In every job or social situation, I found myself being tested not only by the tasty food options before me but also by the skeptical eye of those around me waiting to see if I was for real or not. Even people who just assumed I was Jewish by birth always waited in anticipation of my food eating decisions.

I once – *once* – agreed to a pizza covered in like five kinds of meat with my friends and to this day they still point out that I ate pork *then* so it really isn't an air-tight rule, now is it? I have often been corrected when I say *'Oh, I can't eat that'* with *'No. You choose to not eat it.'* Somehow my entire relevancy as a Jew is dependent on a perfectly clean slate, or I suppose a perfectly clean plate. No level of kosher is acceptable for these people either. If I pass the no-pork test and wiggle through the seafood issue suddenly someone has discovered something on my plate that touched something non-kosher or has pig foot gel in it. Gleefully they point it out and wait as if I will begin screaming and melt into a puddle of goo before them.

To make matters worse other Jews in public seem to think it's no big deal to eat that big hunk of ham in front of everybody not realizing (or caring) that they have just disqualified all of us in the 'true Jew' Olympics. I can honestly say that in every social scenario in which people have offered me food and I have politely declined because of kosher reasons I have heard *'I know so and so and they are Jewish and they eat this.'*

There is a Rabbinic idea around being kosher that says the sin is not only eating the unclean food item itself but also doing so in front of non-Jews who will judge all Jews for it. They are absolutely correct too. Goys never forget. My wise Jewish friends who are kosher have explained to me that it's best to just politely decline the food without a reason. People will think it could be anything from rudeness to a food allergy. If I knew then what I know now I would agree, but remember that a great span of time was dedicated to my need to prove I was-too Jewish to everyone who made eye contact.

Truth be told they are right. Kosher rules are so complex and so difficult that it's impossible to explain it to non-Jews without stumbling over yourself. I generally like to educate people on Jewish topics but unfortunately this one has the unique distinction of not really having a good 'why' associated with it. *'I can eat giraffe but not catfish'* always causes a raised eyebrow and then an earnest *'why?'* You'd think that *'Because I'm Jewish'* would be good enough for our PC world afraid of offending anyone, but even a *'Because G-d said so'* does not satisfy them on this question. They want to know *why* I can't eat this or that. It makes no sense!

Some excitedly jump into a game of *'Ok, but what if...'* where they construct the most absurd scenario possible just to see where your line in the sand is. *'Ok, but what if you were on a desert island and your only option was seal and giraffe but you didn't have anything to hunt to giraffe with...'* Others like to begin running through a comprehensive list of all the animals and creatures on Earth to see which you can and cannot eat. Pause for a moment when answering and they look at you like they finally cracked and debunked your entire philosophy on the spot. Ha! They knew it was all nonsense. Actually, it's more like telling people you don't eat any grains, carbs or animal products except for blue corn and chicken skin left to bake in the sun for precisely 14 hours during the full moon.

The more annoying, I mean *inquisitive*, ones will also then point out that if I do some stuff I'm not supposed to do but hold tight to this or that kosher rule isn't that the exact same thing as being a dirty lying hypocrite? You got me. Jesus was right all along. Attempting to explain the depth of Jewish understanding of sin is literally impossible in a 10-minute social conversation about why you won't eat their baked beans.

The laws of Kashrut do not have reasons. There is no explanation for them at all. No significance or reward/punishment is described either. The Oral and Written law simply say that you must not eat certain things and the Rabbis have been detailing it down to bread crumbs ever since. We do it because we are Jews and that's really it, yet it is such a defining part of our public persona.

People know Jews don't eat certain things and they seem to find this offensive and contradictory. I find that fascinating. No one asks me why I wear my kippah all the time instead of, say, a bowler hat. No one questions why our official symbol is the Star of David and not the smiley face. People are perfectly comfortable with the idea that I work on Friday nights even though it's the Sabbath and they do not discount my entire religion for it, but lord help me if I eat a non-kosher jelly bean.

To make matters more complicated, I don't really eat kosher at all. I abstain from certain food groups like most seafood and pork but I still live out of vending machines and eat from fast food places. I honestly cannot defend myself, or most Jews I know for that matter, on our eating habits. The 'Jews eating Chinese food on Christmas' thing is not an isolated joke. Eating kosher is hard and in many ways, feels impossible. I know that Russian Jews living in the middle of ice plains persecuted in the 15th century or whatever managed, but it's not that easy for me.

I cannot even begin to describe what eating kosher really is either. I own a book[80] that is about 800 pages long devoted to just cooking and eating kosher in your home. If you are serious about it then you do not eat goy-food at all and that means no Taco Bell. Products purchased in the store must have a kosher label and the right kind of kosher label and then there is the cooking utensil thing. Meat and milk cannot mix so anything that touches milk cannot be used for meat and vice versa. That requires different cooking pots, utensils and plates. For Passover, you have to have an entire other set of dishes that also meet the no meat and milk rule. Shabbat has its own plate system too.

I buy mostly cheap Tupperware and plastic utensils because I'm lazy and do not like washing dishes.

That is just at home. If you venture outside of your house you have to make sure the whole milk and meat thing is observed as well as both sets never touching anything treif. It's just not possible. Well it is possible, I'm just lazy.

There is no good excuse for why I have never adopted strict kosher rules outside of the fact that it is so overwhelming and complicated and it really is an all or nothing thing if you go 100%. You drop that milk spoon in the meat pot and it's over with. They are not kidding. But that is for the Orthodox. Being a Conservative leaning Jew I find myself more in the 12-step plan of being kosher. I feel there are kosher levels and I am about a level 2. I do not eat pork or non-kosher seafood. I do still eat milk and meat together but I try to stay mindful of it as much as possible but that is about as far as I reasonably feel I can go right now.

My Jewish family is like kosher level 5 because they have different plates and pots and they buy packages with kosher symbols on them but even our Chassidic rabbi can't eat anything cooked there. They are the most kosher people I know too. I am the 2nd most kosher person I know unfortunately. Reform communities are sadly not very interested in kosher standards. But no one really intentionally eats non-kosher as a statement that I am aware of. It is more of a cultural curiosity they do not hold as necessary.

I feel like kosher is one of those rabbi-is-a-challah things the rabbis warned us about. Food has always been used in ritual meals and so one of the speculations about our very strict dietary laws is that it was meant to keep us together and away from socializing with idolaters who could convert people away as they so often did. Kosher laws are not, however, a food health thing as many people claim. It has nothing to do with the plague or bad disease carrying pork or shrimp. G-d wants us to be kosher because He said so.

Kosher seems to be a very touchy subject around Jews too. I always thought it would be very team-player like where people would jump in to save others who were about to eat something non-kosher but it seems to be more of a 'don't ask, don't tell' situation. People eat as they please and no one says anything about it. It is unusual for Jews to do that. The only exception to this seems to be Jews who are hostile to kosher-eating Jews. This I have experience first-hand. There have been times when I ordered in a restaurant and asked for specifics like no bacon or cheese and have gotten a dismissive smirk or even an earful of how silly it all is.

I feel like so many Jews find rebelling against kosher rules as a strange freedom like sneaking out of their window at night past curfew. They seem to like to break the rule just because it's there and they don't like to be reminded of it either. Even dinners at the synagogue sometime cause complaints when people insist on kosher food items and others dismiss it as nonsense. I get why men don't wear tzizt or kippahs in public in a small community but I honestly don't understand the hostility to mild ambivalence towards this practice. For me I have always felt it was just the nature of my status that being kosher was so overwhelming and I assumed I would grow into it over time but for many it seems to be a nice option they take on holidays if anything.

Where kosher used to be the only way to eat it is now a luxury item used to distinguish a particularly nice meal for a particularly important holiday. People serve kosher food at big events or at large gatherings as a status symbol almost, but in everyday life it seems to just be viewed as unnecessary.

All joking aside though I do feel some of the most insecurity in my Jewish life when it comes to how I eat. I do not always make good choices when I am on my own as there is no one to notice if I mess up and I am fortunate to have a best friend who is very cautious about looking at menus and ensuring I do not accidentally order something I'm not supposed to eat. I admit sometimes it annoys the heck out of me too when I really want something and she points it out. I would have gotten away with eating it if it weren't for her pesky inspection techniques! But like all things I feel there is a greater purpose for the smallest things

I choose to do with my day. Eating is one of the most simple and significant things one does every single day.

On a practical note, Judaism does not punish in an all or nothing fashion. Judaism doesn't really punish at all. The loss comes from not fulfilling the commandment itself whereas the joy comes from fulfilling it. When you prepare a meal with such precision you appreciate it far more than if you just stop by someplace and plop whatever was on sale on a plate. Each kosher choice you make is a little checkmark. Every time I eat I have the opportunity to choose to be kosher or not. I do my best to make the best choice I can with what I have. While kosher is a yes or no question on all foods, it is also about making small choices. So, I choose the chicken sandwich instead of the cheeseburger and it brings me a step closer that day.

Up there with *'What's that thing on your head?'* and *'So Jews just don't believe in Jesus, right?'* is *'Hey, can Jews eat this?'* Although I find it annoying sometimes I am kind of grateful for the constant paparazzi-esque stance non-Jews keep around me whenever I eat in front of them. I know myself well enough that if people didn't notice I would eat just about anything depending on my level of interest and effort that day. Knowing that I am watched makes me make better choices because I do not just speak for myself but now I speak, well eat, for all Jews.

Yes, I am one of *those* people. In any gathering, there is always that one person who has special dietary needs that ruins everything for everybody. Sometimes they are vegans or sometimes they have wheat allergies, whatever the case they force the non-picky people to make more complicated choices about where and what to eat. Surrounded by non-Jews who love all the foods I am forbidden to eat makes it harder. Fortunately, they love me and they always make a point to have a special meal option just for me. They never fail to bring it up either.

Being kosher is unlike other Jewish practices in that it is not limited to your personal experience inside the home or shul. What you eat affects everybody. Every time my friends go out to eat they can pretty much pick anything off of the menu but I have to find something and pick it apart to make sure its edible and try to ignore the fact that its likely going to be cooked on the same stove the other's food will be. As polite and quiet as I try to be I am never allowed to get away with it either. My friends will sometimes verbally go over my available options with me pointing out the limited items I can choose from and then loudly announce that my food has arrived and double check to just make sure.

I am a private person in many ways and eating has always been a thing I do not talk about. Eating with others has always been a struggle anyways because I tend to be very slow and I eat very little at a sitting. So not only it is awkward that everyone is completely finished and I have barely gotten through my salad but I always take food home and that is always amusing to everyone else. The fact that I need to comb through the menu as if I might pick the poison drink by mistake doesn't ease the tension.

Also, as I have tested out various levels of being kosher over the years, the explaining becomes tedious and embarrassing. *'Yes, now I am not eating milk with meat I know that I did last week.'* With many things in Judaism you find that once you begin something, stopping it is far more noticeable. Some of my friends are very supportive and others just think it's all silly. Some, over the years, have found it humorous to spike my punch by giving me non-kosher things intentionally and then laughing after I have eaten them. There is no polite way to explain that this is not funny. I have found myself in difficult social situations though where I felt like my personal choice of what I planned to eat and what I planned to not eat conflicted with the enjoyment of those who invited me.

I was invited to go to a birthday dinner for one of my friends at a new restaurant that I had no information about except that it was Asian and they cooked the food in front of you. People seem to like that sort of thing. Personally, I prefer to believe my food comes from a replicator and just appears neatly on my plate. I went because everyone was going and it was a birthday dinner and it's just what you do.

My first realization of impending doom was that the rice was all pork-fried and they did not list white rice on the menu. The second was when they came out to cook our food they literally had piles of various meats all mushed together on a single plate. The chicken, fish, ham and shrimp were all mingled together. Third, they were dumped onto the stove thing and separated with the same cooking tools and served one at a time.

Nothing about this experience was kosher but it's not like I could really do or say anything without turning my friend's birthday dinner into the 'day Chad couldn't eat anything.' I decided that I would busy myself in conversation, picture taking and gift giving and no one would notice that I would just take the food home. I took most of the food home anyways normally. My plan was working except that my friends did notice I wasn't eating anything and after some probing I explained the levels of horror I had just witnessed and some looked concerned and others dismissed it as silly and then we were interrupted by the chef who decided to initiate one of restaurant's features: tossing food at you to see if you can catch it in your mouth. He tossed a piece of shrimp directly at my face and I ducked instinctively and it landed in my friend's gift bag.

And then…

I once was invited to a Thanksgiving dinner at the family of my boyfriend who did not understand what a Jew was at all. I was a last-minute addition since some of the family disapproved of him bringing me but once it was settled I just understood it would be a typical tense family-style dinner as I was always used to. When I arrived and an eternity of time between then and eating I found that literally every item they served incorporated pork in some way.

The turkey was wrapped in bacon. The stuffing, mashed potatoes, corn and beans all had ham in them. The biscuits were cooked using the leavings from the bacon used on the turkey. I was already a controversial guest and had already had several awkward *'So you're Jewish…'* questions asked and now I was going to have to sit through a meal with absolutely nothing I could eat. There are very few things as absolutely horrible as sitting at a stranger's table and politely declining to eat, you know anything they offer.

Fortunately, my boyfriend was feisty and confrontational and chose to use this as the reason for leaving early. It was still horrible for me because I do not like to be rude and under any classification I felt this was rude but he took most of the blame by grabbing my hand and storming out.

I noticed a huge difference in my perception of eating shortly after my conversion was complete. The considerations I always had about maintaining a good image still apply, but now it's more about what I do for myself too. I mean why would you go through this entire process, get your papers and then sit down to a ham sandwich? The journey doesn't end when you convert. In fact, everything I did before was just practice.

When I make food choices today I feel this deep obligation to not only G-d and my people but also myself. I worked hard for this and I don't want to screw it up now! Every bite I take is a constant reminder of the choice I made and the new life I now have. No more cheating. It's strange to think that something as simple as eating could have such a huge impact on your emotional and religious well-being, but the truth is being kosher is just one small thing a Jew does every day to show respect and love for G-d.

12

Pink Diamonds

When I was growing up I learned of a story that said when you died and went to Heaven G-d, or Jesus, would give you a crown. The crown would have stones representing the people you had saved while on Earth. Each stone type and color represented a different category of person you saved. Catholics were like emeralds and Hindus were opals and of course, Jews were diamonds. Everyone wanted to save a Jew. What do you get if you save a Gay Jew? A pink diamond. Duh.

Being gay is one of the most fascinating aspects of being Jewish. When I first began, I found myself reassured by the very open perspective that I saw from the Jewish community on homosexuality. I quickly met several gay Jews, two of whom had been married by a rabbi and as far as I could tell no one gave it a second glance. This was very important to me because I had really lost my faith in Christianity largely over my sexuality. After years of struggle I found not having to explain myself to be very comforting. Lesbians[81] were not mentioned in the Torah as they were a strictly New Testament thing and there were only two versus in the entire book that mentioned men. One of which basically said it wasn't such a big deal. Reform rabbis agreed that the requirement to build a family and live a Jewish life could be easily accomplished in a same-sex household.

I remember my grandmother's husband even asking me if the only reason I was doing this was because they let you be gay. I would strut around with a sense of incredible accomplishment stating that *my religion* was fine with me being gay. In my social interactions, no Jewish person ever questioned it. I felt I had finally found my place in the world. Back then I felt strongly that Jewish experience was entirely up to my own design and so being gay was just part of how I would do Judaism.

In all honestly, I never thought of myself without putting *gay* right at the front of my identity and for much of time that is still true today. Even if I felt it was completely against the faith I, at the time, wouldn't have thought twice about questioning it. I believed that being pro-gay was more important than anything else I could stand for. Today I see my sexuality as just another aspect of my personal experience that doesn't really impact my life one way or the other. It certainly doesn't impact my Jewish experience. But, as in all things, there is a Jewish opinion on the subject. Many of them.

The pagan world was filled with all manner of behavior with very little regard to morality as we understand it today. Their gods were highly human, highly sexual and highly unethical. Pagan cultures typically incorporated sex in a dual reproduction/pleasure manner in their lives. Women were for romance and babies, men were for pleasure. Young boys were used as sexual servants and men showed dominance over one another via rape. This was common place in the areas where Judaism grew.

The first commandment was to *"be fruitful and multiply."*[82] As such Jews have always considered large families to be a blessing. The stories in the Torah often described being childless as the worst thing that could happen and G-d giving a child was an incredible blessing.

Circumcision was the first pact with G-d and Abraham to distinguish his children from the rest of the world. Jews were meant to be the priests to the world and be a beacon of light and hope showing a better way, but only Jews were required to follow the commandments.

When you look traditionally at the culture what you see are Jews separating themselves to such an extent that they would be obviously different from other peoples. It seemed G-d wanted this for a reason, so that those peoples could view Jews as good and to live by their example. As such, Jewish men were required to marry Jewish women and begin large Jewish families. Every single thing in Judaism revolves around the family.

Also, in Judaism men are considered to be in need of more control than women who are considered to be more spiritually evolved. This is why Jewish men have more strict rules than women do. It is also why women are not mentioned in the Torah in terms of homosexuality. Men in the area were accustomed to male homosexual activity, so on a cultural level it made sense to contrast yourself from a sexually liberal culture by being sexually exclusive. Sex, however, in Judaism is a very holy thing as it is the closest act to G-d's own creation ability. Because of this symbolism, it was to be highly respected and sacred.

The 613 commandments are meant to be difficult, but achievable. They are designed to build a life where literally every action is significant with G-d in mind. No Jew is exempt from these laws. So, an Orthodox Rabbi asked about same-sex attraction once said to me: *'So you're gay, you still have to follow the commandments.'* In other words, it doesn't matter what obstacles you have in front of you, you must fulfill your duty not only to G-d and your people, but to the world. Also, in Judaism it is not all or nothing. When I told an Orthodox Rabbi I was gay he said, *'Well, 612, out 613 ain't bad.'* It may be a struggle, but I have an obligation to keep the laws even if some of them are more difficult than others.

Here is my opinion on the subject: my challenge and obligation is to obey the laws G-d gave me. I need to adapt my life to fit his vision for me. It is not my job to be a lawyer and find loopholes that will allow me to squeeze through. I have no right to take away from G-d his vision for my life by choosing a path that separates me from everything he has planned.

If I choose to be an observant Jew then I need to do my best to follow all of the laws, not just the easy ones. I am not an observant Jew, but I respect those who are and I respect and honor the laws. I just know that I am not strong enough to complete them as I should. I do not reject them. I feel like each mitzvah; each commandment, is important and valuable and I believe in them. I think that whenever you perform one a spark of light shoots into the sky to light up the world. I think that G-d knew what he was doing when he separated us from the rest of the people and asked us to live unique lives. I don't think changing it to suit our needs has been very successfully either.

Now, this is not the end of the discussion either. I spoke with a Chassidic and an Orthodox rabbi and they both confirmed that homosexuality isn't nearly as clean cut as 'just don't do it.' Not everyone in Traditional Judaism feels a gay man should attempt to override his feelings and get married. Some even find this to be counterproductive to the goals G-d set. It is often described as saying that even if you are sympathetic to the experience of a gay person, you cannot condone it through Jewish law.

Judaism is less interested in the reasons you do not follow the commandments and is more interested in helping you find ways to incorporate more into your life. It is true that being gay is fairly insignificant in terms of your place in Jewish life; it is just that an Orthodox rabbi cannot override the Torah to say its ok either. I find personally that part of accepting Judaism means understanding that even though my sexuality may not be approved of, it's not rejected either. I cannot expect an Orthodox rabbi to marry me to a man but I appreciate that he or she never questions to involve me in Jewish ritual. Ironically, being gay is really the last thing any rabbi is going to be concerned about in terms of my Jewish life.

In my community, there are many active gay Jews and my rabbi is open and comfortable with Jewish same-sex marriage. I support her and my community and I love the people who live in it. Building a Jewish life isn't about what you give up but what in Judaism you add. Personally, I am comfortable being a gay man. I went through a period of considering an Orthodox lifestyle which would complicate my sexual preferences and I am HIV+ so marrying a woman, regardless of my level of observance, would be unrealistic.

But over the years I have come to realize there is no grand virtue in denying yourself happiness to suit a larger purpose or authority. My rabbi, my other two rabbis, every Jewish person I know, every Jewish person I have ever spoken to regardless of observance and my friends and family accept me just as I am. So why worry about something that matters to no one else? Would I get married today in a Jewish wedding? Absolutely. Why? Because my community celebrates it and I respect and celebrate Judaism. Why deny myself a joyous moment when it simply isn't necessary.

13

Sabbath Bride

Shabbat is confusing. First of all, wiccans also have "Shabbats" and there is a band called "Black Sabbath" and of the things we could disagree on, Muslims, Jews and Christians decided that *'Keep the Sabbath day holy'* was absolutely vital to our religious experience, we just couldn't decide on the same day. Shabbat was also my most anxiety-driven anticipation when I first decided to become Jewish.

Reading about Shabbat and what could not be done I found myself overwhelmed. The conversion books sort of talked about Shabbat in fluffy poetic terms that made it sound like a nice weekly holiday where people got together and talked about happy memories and such but everything else described it as what I interpreted to mean a day where you couldn't do anything but sit still and wait for it to be over. It took me many years to understand the significance of this weekly event and to be honest it is still much of a mystery.

The first problem is that many Jews don't pay any attention to it and they didn't on TV either. Adam Sandler never talked about Shabbat in his movies and as with my first temple experience, Jews drove and ate and worked and cooked and all kinds of things on this holy day. Well first it took me a while to grasp the concept that a Jewish day is sundown to sundown so it might as well be two days. No one talked about Shabbat or the Sabbath or Shabbos in the same fluffy terms as the books did and besides going to the synagogue and singing about it, there wasn't much else.

I was confused because I pictured Jews frantically racing around to get indoors, get everything set up and then as the last hue of orange disappeared from the sky, I imagined everyone would fall into the living room floor and patiently wait until the next day. That did not happen. Well I understand that happens in Israel but that didn't happen here. For most of my Jewish experience Shabbat was just the question non-Jews asked me about when they saw me working on Friday nights.

I didn't really experience a Shabbat until I had my first dinners with my Jewish family. On Friday nights, they would invite me over and it was surreal. While I did drive there and they did cook, most of the cooking was done beforehand and things were just heating up. While she would go and light candles he would set the table and then together we would sing, pray, wash hands and then eat what I thought was a huge meal but was small in comparison to some, only three courses!

Watching her light candles became a fascinating thing for me because it held this moment of spirituality and history that can only be witnessed live. You don't take pictures on Shabbat so the only way to experience the moment is to see it. She covers her hair and in a private moment prays over the candles. There is this peaceful glow and the air just freezes for a time before the busy preparation begins again. In that time when everything stops and she prays I feel the spirit of what Shabbat was always described to me in books.

We pray and cut the Challah and we sing and eat salad, soup and chicken. It's this reuniting feeling of what family always felt like in my mind. The topics are wonderful and we talk sometimes late into the night before everyone shuffles off to bed. It's not a normal dinner at all and the mood is so familiar and cozy. It feels like what you see in paintings of Jewish families.

I feel like Shabbat is multifaceted. On the very practical side it is this weekend time where you don't work and you leave the household chores for the next day. You eat and just enjoy the luxury of doing so while you banter with your family and enjoy this miniature vacation. It's also holy, of course, but that feels more subtle and individual. It is almost as if the spirit G-d blessed the day with lives in the family bonding together rather than a ritual or outside source. It is simple and beautiful in all of its perceived complication.

I think it's the complication that makes people lose sight of the beauty. People so often think of all the things they cannot do that they give up and treat it as any normal day when all they need to do is just stop and experience it. The stopping is the hard part. It is not full of ritual or complicated prayers and steps, the difficult aspect is the idea that you just stop and sit down. It's like trying to be quiet, it can be impossible sometimes. I imagine that would be the point maybe. When we quiet our lives, we can perceive them more clearly.

I have to say that I have never really experienced a Shabbat myself alone. I don't know if it is possible or not. It feels as though you need a family in order to make it work. Alone you don't share or express anything, you just stay quiet. I am selfish and I get so bored without my many electronics that I have never really been able to enjoy it myself outside of my Jewish family. I wonder if that was also G-d's point. The Sabbath is the day He rested from His work, maybe He didn't want to do it alone either.

14

Sacred Israel

A Jew cannot be neutral on the topic of Israel. Every Jew has a strong opinion about Israel including me, but this was not always the case. Actually, for the first several years of my Jewish journey I was absolutely *meh* on the whole topic. I grew up Christian and the fancy kind too where people sing and dance and sometimes speak in tongues. Israel was where everything in the Bible happened and where Jesus was planning to return and build a New Jerusalem that was to come out of the sky, roughly. It might as well have been Narnia to me. It just sort of always was and I was sure would always be.

I do remember furrowing my eyebrows a bit when I heard about the *creation* of Israel in 1948 since clearly anyone with a bible knows Israel has always been there. The Middle East peace thing was just a storybook concept meant to fulfill a prophecy of it ending one day and bringing on the Rapture. Honestly, I don't remember thinking of it in any other terms. I managed to get all the way to college without a single independent thought on the nature of this primary part of human history and the central destiny of all Jews. My grandmother traveled there with her church in the 1970's and took lots of rocks and things with her on her way back but always described it as being 'too dangerous' to visit again. Her religious TV shows also went on and on about "The Holy Land" as well but I just thought they were being poetic. It wasn't until I experienced my first attack for being Jewish that I developed a sense of what Israel means to Jews.

I was in my last year at college, which after 6 years was a pretty big accomplishment, and I had carefully designated myself the standard issue class gay and Jew. Any topic in either category would be officially mediated by me. I was president of the Jewish Student Association too but we only had a few students and never had any meetings and I was also active in the Yiddish choir at the time. Those bits are all important.

During my years in college I had taken many Arabic classes and made friends with many Muslim students. I was still wary of Christians in large part and I mumbled angrily whenever I saw them painting their various messages about salvation and love on the sidewalks. 'Hate speech' I believe I called it. I was comfortably finding my place with Jews and whenever the topic of Israel came up I usually listened politely but didn't really provide any input myself. I didn't really *have* any input myself. Actually, I believe my position on the topic was that fighting over land was silly and if the Arabs wanted it so badly why didn't we just pick everything up and move it to someplace safe and not surrounded by tribal conflicts, like Utah or something.

One day I was checking my Facebook and I received an invitation to an event titled something like "Peace in the Middle East and Israel." They were to show a documentary called *Occupation 101*[83] and would have speakers in a panel format. One of my Muslim friends had invited me to it. I was terrified. First of all, I assumed that since I would be the only Jew in the audience that I would be expected to discuss the Israel side and I didn't know enough to even begin that sort of discussion. I knew that I supported Israel because I was Jewish but that is pretty much where it ended for me.

My Muslim friend then began posting lots of status updates about the 2009 Gaza war[84] and how many innocent children and babies Israel had intentionally murdered. I read them in horror as I honestly did not know many details myself and also because I suddenly realized I would have to speak to this. How do I defend Israel murdering hundreds of babies and children? I decided to share this event with my fellow Jews at the next Yiddish choir meeting at dinner and see what they thought and oh did I ever release a shit storm.

Ok, so somehow I had just missed the intense and passionate emotions surrounding Israel by these people because the moment I brought this up I was inundated with a frantic display that was so dramatic I have nothing to compare it to in any previous experience. Everyone was angry and concerned and demanding justice for what was surely to be a horror display on anti-Semitism at our very own school. I just didn't get it. I thought this was going to be a panel discussion on the various sides of the issue, I didn't see where the anger and concern was coming from. I just wanted some nuggets of information so that I could intelligently answer questions if asked.

Oh no. I had just opened a Pandora's Box and there was nothing I could to do stop it. I learned in the span of an hour that *Occupation 101* was a propaganda film designed to insight anti-Israel and anti-Jewish hatred and that it was false in its entirety. I learned that these sort of events were happening on campuses across the nation and Pro-Israel groups were being constantly attacked as well as Jewish students.[85] I also learned that being Pro-Israel was far more than just a cause for these people.

I worked a night job at the time so it allowed me hours of free time on the internet and that night I decided to watch this film and read up about the Israel thing. By morning my entire world had been turned up-side-down. I had always just assumed that the images of Israeli soldiers pointing guns at terrified children and such were a result of war. I thought it was horrible but to me it blended into a series of war images that were all terrible. I didn't really think Israel was 'ethnically cleansing' the Palestinians but I did think it was kind of mean to block them off into a ghetto and blow them up.

I learned in those few hours of research that my entire worldview on this had been incorrect. Israel was not killing innocent people; the Palestinians were putting innocent people directly in harm's way and then using their deaths to rile up even more violence. The children were often causalities of literally being placed in front of buildings where bombs were to be set off. They built their rocket launchers in schools and playgrounds intentionally to claim Israel was attacking children when they were actually trying to destroy the weapons constantly being used to terrorize Israelis. They even warned the Palestinians as to the precise time and day the attacks would happen. That is how they knew to put their children there!

Israel was not founded on the blood and pain of terrified native peoples being driven from their ancient homeland with swords and guns; it was actually purchased from transient landowners and governments. "Palestinian" was a title similar to a "North American" in relevance to ethnicity or peoplehood. The area known as Palestine also included Jordan which, when also divided into a new country, the people inside became Jordanians rather than "Palestinian refugees." Somehow only the Arabs currently living in the boundaries of Israel at the time were "Palestinian refugees." No one in Jordan was demanding a "right of return" to their "homeland" of "Palestine" in Jordan.

Jews from around the world began to immigrate to Israel and built it into a thriving and bountiful beacon of hope and powerful positive influence to the world where it had been little more than sand and history previously. They had given concession after concession to try and "make peace" and each time the Palestinians refused or started some new war. The media insisted on painting Israel as the big mean oppressor and the Palestinians as helpless native people being tormented for fun.[86] My mind was literally blown wide open. I had no idea something like this could really happen.

In my new yet still very naïve knowledge of the situation I assumed that any discussion of the facts would render the anti-Israel argument moot. I mean you can't argue with facts and history, right? We had about a week to prepare for the event which was being sponsored by the University's Liberal Arts department and several professors were involved in the panel. Our rabbi, who was also a professor, was not invited or even informed of the event. We spoke to the dean of the department, the President of the university and anyone else that we thought would help us in this event. While the participants in the event felt it was a harmless exercise in debate and discussion, others disagreed and we were able to get a second event the following week to show a different film of our choosing.

In that week, my world on campus itself also dramatically shifted. I found that all of my Muslim friends had suddenly turned against me over this issue. I can disagree with a friend over same-sex marriage or abortion and we can still hang out and have dinner, I found that I was either for or against Muslims as a whole in supporting Israel. My Muslim friends demanded that I speak for them or I would be forever labeled a baby-killing Islamophobic bigot Zionist. I was so frustrated and emotionally destroyed and I felt that I was literally choosing my future in how I would see the world and interact with people again. I realized I could never go back to the 2-dimensional view of everyone living in happiness and joy with friendly disagreements.

The evening of the event was chaotic. We had printed out informational fliers and found ourselves standing in the doorway with people streaming in being handed fliers from both sides and being frantically shouted at as to whom they should believe. The chaos increased as Muslim students and community individuals began trying to force only their views and their fliers into the stream of people. We retaliated by rushing into the room and filling every seat with our information. I have never seen anger and hatred from people before like I did that night when Muslims I called friends shouted at me that I was a baby-killer and supported genocide.

The representative of the Liberal Arts Department, I believe she was the associate Dean or something, set the stage for the discussion by stating that sometimes people can resort to many levels when they have no other options for freedom and that this can be expressed in suicide bombings. Realizing that she had just publicly defended and even justified suicide bombings woke me up that this was not going to be a fair and open discussion at all.

I had already seen the film so it was merely an exercise in tense anticipation and a growing sense of worry as I watched the reactions from the non-Muslim individuals who had decided to come for the event. Women in hijabs sobbed openly and the panel just shook their heads in disgust. We were watching a Holocaust documentary and I was expected to defend the Nazis it seemed. Despite the fact – actual fact – that everything stated in the video was provably wrong, the panel discussed it as being a good and fair representation of events.

While one Sociology professor admitted, it was clearly propaganda he failed to point out that not a single scene, interview or declaration made had even a falsified subtitle to state where it had occurred or even when the interview was done. It was literally just a fluid stream of crying Palestinians and images of things blowing up with commentary on the imaginary genocide that had yet to be successful in over 60 years.

Our event had less chairs set out in preparation which I think was intentional but admittedly did not draw as many people. Most of the people there had attended the first event and not a single person sat with arms uncrossed. We watched a moderate documentary called *The Case for Israel* by Alan Dershowitz[87]. The video, like all Pro-Israel discussion, was designed to provide factual information in a fair and balanced way which included negative information about Israel which could be debated if need be. No one cried during this one and the panel, made up of the same individuals, merely agreed that it too was a propaganda film on equal grounds with the previous one.

Somehow in my college experience I had grown accustomed to the idea that fair discussion was the norm. I grew accustomed to this because that is what my liberal professors always said they were doing before presenting only their side. I realized that truth and facts were not enough. The other side had thrown mud on us and we were desperately trying to clean it up.

Unfortunately, many people decided that looking dirty was the same as being dirty. Since this event we formed a group to work with Christians in the area in order to react with more public support if another anti-Israel event were to take place on our campus. We founded the Coalition of Friends for Israel of West Virginia.[88] There have been other panel discussions there and at other colleges in the area but so far nothing has escalated to the same level as this one was. Perhaps we made it clear that a reaction would occur and simple slander would not be met with anything less.

Since then I have helped organize multiple large public Israel Independence Day events in our city and gone to several AIPAC (American Israel Political Action Committee) conferences in Washington DC. I have written a children's book titled: *Ronni, The Little Jewish Girl Who Loved Israel*[89] which features a young girl working in her community to bring information about and support for Israel. I now have a well-founded and legitimate perspective on the subject even if some in the Jewish community find it to be a bit extreme. I am Pro-Israel and I see no other reason not to be.

Being Pro-Israel is strange in our community. So many Jews take on the view that we must look at all sides and allow everyone's perspective to have equal value. That sounds nice on paper but it doesn't work if the other perspective's primary goal is your destruction. Anti-Israel groups are not interested in open discussion that covers all sides. They are focused on destroying Israel completely and they do so with no hesitation. Often a panel discussion will consist of people who demand the absolute destruction of Israel for its brutal crimes against humanity and people who disagree. We rarely seem to have an equal balance on the other side demanding the actual good Israel does and pointing out the constant lies coming from the opposition.

If you want to hear people talk about Israel with confidence and unflinching passionate exuberance you have to go to a church. What is interesting is that even with my strong position on the topic; my rabbi who is very moderate on the topic considers it a positive balance to the discussion. As of this writing[90] three Jewish teenagers were kidnapped and murdered by Palestinians in Israel and an Arab Israeli appears to have been murdered in Israel in retribution by Jewish extremists. The dialogue in my Jewish community ranges from deep mourning of the three Jewish teenagers to out spoken demands that Jewish terrorism and Islamic terrorism are identical in nature and the only solution is to open more discussion to try and find common ground.

The reality is that there is no consensus in the Jewish community over how to view Israel. Jewish liberals strongly conflict with Jewish conservatives and moderates are forever trying to find bridges to meet the two. If you are not particularly interested or comfortable with political discussion, being Jewish just isn't for you. I would like to tell you with utter confidence that you can go by my word alone, but you will find a dozen Jews who adamantly demand I am wrong and another dozen who agree with me completely. Supporting Israel is not nearly as straight forward as you might assume it to be.

15

The Jesus Thing

Yes, the Jesus thing. When you convert to Judaism the one thing no one talks about is how you deal with your former religion. It feels like everyone expects you to start from a blank slate when you walk in the door. For some people this is true, but for me it certainly was not. I have mentioned that I was intensely Christian in my childhood to teen years. This is not an exaggeration. I was religious to the point that people worried about me. Even other Christians sometimes raised an eyebrow at me. I wasn't crazy, I was just passionate. But part of this passion was an overwhelming need to compensate for a deep inner sense that something wasn't right.

I grew up floating between Baptist, Nazarene and Pentecostal styles of Christianity. They are all similar in their charismatic approach to religious expression but are as different as can be in all other areas. Even their basic concept of Jesus and G-d are different. One thing they do have in common, however, is passion. They are very passionate people. Worship services are exciting, filled with loud fast music and people losing normal control over polite body language and verbal expression.

I can remember being a child and sobbing violently at the altar with a line of people around me singing, crying and raising their arms into the sky begging for revelation and forgiveness. I wasn't sobbing because I felt the spirit or because I was overwhelmed by a message from G-d. I was sobbing because I wasn't. I never felt what the others expressed to the extent they did. I would sit there with my head in my hands waiting to *feel* like I had been saved.

Ironically in hindsight if I had not fully believed in the concept of accepting Jesus I don't think I would have been so emotionally distraught. At the time, however, I felt empty and afraid. I was always afraid. 'Always Afraid' is a good way to describe my childhood actually. Religiously this was, of course, a fear of Hell which was omnipresent in everything we did. Sure, people sang and celebrated Jesus, but they also warned of Hell. They warned of Hell a lot. My relationship with Jesus was much more of me begging him to prove to me that I wasn't going to go to Hell rather than a deep friendship or love as described by everyone else. I did not really feel him or experience a spiritual fulfillment when talking about him. I was actually trying so hard to force those things that I would always leave feeling beaten and alone.

As a result, I read and prayed and talked about Jesus more than I did anything else from about age 8 to 14.

Everyone thought this was strange. I did not care about the same things other kids did and I was acutely focused on one particular part of Christianity and that was *The Rapture.* Jews don't really know much about this concept which I found stunning to be honest.

From middle school on I was literally prepared every single day for a sudden and massive rapture of people being shot into the clouds accompanied by loud trumpet blasts. If I saw a funny cloud or heard a loud noise or if the air stilled for just a moment I would hold by breath in anticipation. I believed I would be left behind. As strong as I wanted my faith to be, I was tormented by the idea that I was just not good enough to make it into Heaven.

I'm not exactly sure what an 11-year-old can do to fall out of G-d's graces, but I was sure I had done something. It was all very Puritan in that I felt G-d must have selected me for Hell before I was even born and no amount of effort on my part could change that.

Jesus was this gatekeeper whom I needed to convince if I ever wanted to try. Everyone around me seemed content with their relationship to this man, although I admit I never quite understood how he could manage to be so personally involved with all of them simultaneously. We always talked about how we would meet Jesus when we died and I remember wondering how he ever got anything else done. But as my sexuality became more apparent, things began to change.

I was tightly involved with a church in Florida when I lived there and I was only at the very beginning of understanding what being gay even meant. My step-father explained it to me and that I was a homosexual, but all I really understood was that I knew what the Bible said about homosexuality. When I moved back to Ohio to live with my father I no longer had a single church I went to and moving towards my teenage years and beyond my sexuality took a front seat in my world.

Battling my sexuality was sort of the focal point of those years and instead of finding peace within the church I found it to be a terrifying place where I would be judged and rejected. If I felt separated from my Christian peers spiritually before, it did not compare to anything I felt then. Truth be told this was all in my head. The people I engaged with at church never had any clue I was gay and they treated me wonderfully. It was my fear that drove me into constant anxiety.

My faith became my own in many ways as I tried to desperately find a way to understand my feelings and also embrace my religion. I tried many different churches but I continued to feel as though I would be found out at any moment and so I never quite relaxed enough to fit in. I even attempted ex-gay therapy in a church for a while but it felt as though completion was a prerequisite for acceptance there.

As I traveled through my teens and into my 20's I became more and more bitter and angry with Christianity as a whole. I separated Jesus from the church and I began seeking alternative narratives and perspectives that allowed me to keep a relationship with this man while not being bound to what I perceived as Christian bigotry. This is what led me towards more and more abstract spirituality and concepts like reincarnation.

All the while I kept Jesus in the back of my mind and in my prayers, thinking him to be a misunderstood person whom no one really knew. I personified him as a human torn out of his time and placed into mythology. I imagined he was a great spiritual leader or prophet and he never intended anything found in the modern church.

In the meantime, I found Judaism and I admit that in the early years I was really more focused on creating a Jewish identity than dealing with what to do with Jesus. Jesus was Jewish, right? So why couldn't I just keep him and the faith he practiced at the same time? Jesus became a Jewish prophet and a great rabbi to me. I assumed other Jewish people would be perfectly fine as long as he wasn't the "son" of anything.

And then I found Rabbi Tovia Singer[91].

Rabbi Tovia Singer is an orthodox rabbi who founded *Outreach Judaism* and focuses primarily on bringing Jews who converted to Christianity (and other religions) back to Judaism. Since most evangelism comes from Christians his work is dedicated to debunking Christian claims about Jesus and his Jewish connection to the Messiah. Through more than a dozen recorded discussions Rabbi Singer broke down every claim, piece of proof, myth and declaration Christians make to say that Jesus is the Jewish Messiah. Listening to him I began to realize that this man I had held in my imagination since childhood was truly a character created and not even representative of an actual person let alone a holy being.

I learned about Judaism from a unique place I had never had access to before and the sheer force and passion from this man allowed me to see and feel a spirit in Judaism I didn't know existed. There was passion and purpose in Torah and this rabbi lived it and loved it openly. His arguments were convincing and he gave me a solid place to stand with Judaism. He allowed me to understand where to go from where I was.

There isn't really a moment when I abandoned Jesus or dismissed him. There were no long goodbye letters to burn or tearful prayers of remembering. I never once said out loud or even thought something along the lines of *"I reject Jesus."* He just sort of faded away into irrelevancy in terms of my spiritual path. Jews don't talk about Jesus, and so I slowly grew to forget he was ever a significant part of my life. To openly dismiss him or reject him would require believing in him and him having some power or authority in the first place.

Intellectually the experience of transitioning from one religious faith to another is devastating. The pathways and associations one builds from childhood are difficult and sometimes impossible to replace. In many ways that is a blessing. I did not need to find a way to put Jesus into Judaism in order to keep harmony between my before faith and my new faith. I just created new paths around the old ones. He honestly was not involved in the process. Knowing what I do now about Judaism and the Jewish Messiah makes Jesus as absurd as Mohammad as a Jewish prophet. They just don't fit together. He feels little more than Zeus or Thor does in my mind and spirit. I cannot look at the Egyptian god Ra with anymore awe or disgust and rejection than I can Jesus to tell you the truth.

Judaism stands alone and the framework is solid. It cannot be replaced or overridden by later interpretation or other belief systems. When you learn about who Moshiach is and how G-d set things up from Torah, Jesus just seems, well, silly. This isn't a slam on Christianity really; it is just a separate and completely independent religion with absolutely no spiritual connection to Judaism. Jews and pagans formed together to create Christianity long ago and that is where the similarities end. Sharing a common ancestry does not connect us any more than finding out George Bush and Barack Obama do.

As is such I don't think one will really understand or learn if one tries to understand how and why Jesus is *not* something. It is far more impactful to understand what Judaism is and what Torah says about the Messiah and then the differences become clear.

Do I miss Jesus? No. I don't even miss the emotional bond I created or the hope and anticipation that filled my mind as a child. When I see images of him or am caused to think about him I either associate an unpleasant frown or really nothing at all. As strange as it sounds, I really do not have an emotional reaction to the character itself. I frown because I often am prepared to see or hear what I know to be absurd in terms of Jewish belief and I dislike it. I don't really like to see Christians do Jewish things or go on about Jewish sacred events or objects because I know too much to believe they honestly know what they are doing. Even when I know it's not negative or offensive, it's unpleasant for me to experience now.

I had my Beit Din[92] in which I sat before two rabbis and an educated elder of the community in preparation of my conversion. In books about converting I had been expecting to be asked either how I felt about Jesus or if I openly rejected him. I remember when I first read *Choosing a Jewish Life* the author brought this up about openly rejecting Jesus at this event and how converts sometimes struggle so much with this part they cannot continue on. I remember how I worried about actually verbally rejecting Jesus in such a way when I first approached the topic. It seemed so contract-with-the-devil in nature. But as I grew in Judaism I slowly stopped thinking about even stating such a thing. It would be no more difficult or different than stating I rejected the Giant Spaghetti Monster as the creator of the universe.

They never asked that question. While my rabbi has talked about other conversion experiences where people tried to make Jesus into a Jewish prophet or rabbi or anything to hold onto him, she didn't feel it was necessary to deal with that issue with me. I suppose that is a good thing in terms of my relationship with my Jewish community. But I admit it is strange to be here now looking back at how deeply I struggled with something I now don't even blink in concern for. It's not denial of my feelings or atheistic angry rejection, I just found all I need in what G-d gave us in Torah and I don't need Jesus to save me any longer.

16

Jewish Evangelism

Jews do not reach out to non-Jews for conversion, but Jews do reach out to other Jews. There is this idea that when a Jew performs a mitzvah it enriches the whole of Judaism. Getting someone to perform a single mitzvah is a blessing and something Chassidic Jews and Chabad houses across the nation and world strive for. In my own small way, I found that I could merge a dream of mine with that same goal. I always wanted to be an author (ta-da) and a few years ago I chose to embark on my first attempt: a children's book. Something I am endlessly asked about is my kippah or yarmulke (funny little hate I wear.) People in all walks of life and in every single situation imaginable directly ask me about in this simple way: *"What's that thing on your head?"*

I decided to go with two goals in mind, first I would address this humorous if not annoying curiosity by playfully illustrating this phenomenon (and titling it *"What's that Thing on Your Head"*) and second I would address the importance of wearing a kippah in hopes that young Jewish boys would be inspired to do so and thus build a small spark of interest in Jewish learning and practice. Jacob, my main character, who is crudely drawn with a sharpie and colored-in with Microsoft Paint, goes on a short journey to learn about what his kippah is and why he wears it. In the end, he shares this with his friends and it's a big happy multicultural love fest involving balloons.

I followed-up the title with *How's That Thing Stay on Your Head?* which is often the follow-up question once people feel secure in their knowledge of why I wear it. In the second of the series I explored the idea that human intervention can only go so far and sometimes you have to trust G-d when you don't really understand something (hint: G-d may or may not hold your kippah on with His finger. Buy the book to find out!)

I have struggled with the internal Jewish community for a long time in the fact that so many of us allow our kids to decide solely on their own if they want to be Jewish or not. Children do not make good choices when it comes to difficult tasks. Christian kids are different because they are filled with spiritual enthusiasm or a sense of collective stronghold against enemy attacks and Orthodox children are not really given a choice in the matter of their practice since everyone around them does it. It's the Jewish children from the rest of Judaism that seem to be given a mere pat on the back in terms of encouragement. I'm going to get in trouble for saying this I know because

Reform kids do have Sunday school (no felt boards) and many parents do send their kids to Jewish day schools but I think my point circles around why Jewish kids do not embrace what is literally a thousand-year heritage fought and bled for so they can enjoy it.

It saddens me because when I see Judaism I see this rich and full history and religious depth that I would have loved as a child. The rituals, the prayers, the meaning and significance of it all are astounding yet I see so many Jewish kids who seem intent on keeping their Judaism safely inside the temple.

I think part of this is that Jewish children go to school with non-Jews all the time and are rarely treated negatively for it. Their Jewish status can be used as a learning tool for a diversity lesson but other than that it just happens to be their religion. They build full identities outside of being Jewish alone and when they go off to college they enter a world in which being Jewish is just an interesting part of your overall character. We seem to be in a never-ending battle to convince Jewish people that Judaism is pretty nifty and full of life and interest. Jewish enrichment is such a part of our experience now that people assume it is Jewish learning as opposed to a reaction to Jewish disinterest.

I decided to contribute in my own way by creating a children's book called *8 Things You Can Do to Make God Smile Everyday*. I had to spell out "God" because, well, G-d won't come up in search engines and it's confusing. The main character is Freddie (I'm not super creative with names) and his purpose is to show you eight individual commandments every Jewish boy can complete in a single day. The mitzvot involved are simple but impactful and my hope is that a Jewish boy will find it interesting and exciting and believe he can decide for himself since that's what he is always told anyways and begin to integrate small changes to his life. I want his Jewish practice to come from inside of him rather than imposed from the outside.

So far all of my children's books have Jewish themes and I think it is because I see so much in Jewish life that I love and I want kids who are lucky enough to be born into it to really understand that while they are children. I also want their parents to stop taking for granted that their kids will embrace Judaism wholly on their own too. Judaism only takes a single generation to fall apart and so through celebration I also hope for unification as well.

The topic of the Jewish future is ongoing. One of the very first conversations I witnessed by a group of Jews was on this very topic. At the time, they were considering how music would be involved during the High Holy Days and it was viewed as both vital to continue the Reform tradition of having an organ and also to ban use of the organ altogether.

Topics range from inter-faith marriage, kosher kitchens and children's book selections for the library. The underlying concern is that we are always worried that Judaism will die out in the next generation. This seems to be true for all branches even though it is often more vocalized by traditional perspectives.

I really struggled to understand this at first to be honest. When you are a Christian there is an endless supply of potential Christians available. If you want people to join you then you simply make your church more exciting or inviting. Seeking out new Christians is a daily part of many people's experience. But Jews don't like to actively seek out converts. Our numbers are almost entirely made up by our children.

As I mentioned, there really is no incentive to continue on being Jewish in any specific way. In previous and more perilous times, a Jew might choose to become a Christian or Muslim or even an Atheist for purely survival reasons. It would just be easier to marry someone who wasn't Jewish and start a Gentile life where you were considered safe. Today a Jew can be happily Jewish in the U.S. and in much of the world without fear. At the same time, there is no reason to actively focus on Jewishness either. A person can enjoy a range of religious, cultural and social experience as a Jew without ever needing to put themselves at personal risk. Why would they worry about the future of Judaism?

There is a common Jewish idea that people maintain Judaism in spite of those who like to kill us. You are likely to hear the joke *"They killed us, we survived, let's eat!"* as a way to describe Jewish historical experience. This idea seems to assume that we continue being Jews for the sake of proving those who tried to kill us have failed. But younger Jews don't have this understanding. No one is trying to kill us (in the US) and most have spent their lives experiencing their Jewish identity as somewhat of a novelty in their non-Jewish social lives. I have met so many young Jews who strongly identify as Jewish but have no interest in Jewish religious or even social practice at all. Their Jewishness doesn't diminish from their point of view in the least. Even if they marry a non-Jew they assume their children will still be Jewish themselves.

I think this is a cultural thing that is shifting. I understand the concept behind it all but I can't help but feel it is unnecessary in many ways. I quoted the story of the Rabbi who became a challah earlier to illustrate this idea and I agree with it very much, but I also feel it is something that can be avoided. If you teach your children to love Judaism then there will be no reason for them to stray.

Jewish children just don't need to be religiously Jewish if they don't want to. They can travel anywhere in the world and don't need to stay in small, tightly knit communities anymore. Jews don't have to stay together to remain safe or to remain Jewish. A Jew today can build their life anyway they choose and incorporate Judaism in any way they like. Our modern way of thinking precludes ideas of social responsibility in favor of absolute individual freedom. There is no shame in moving across the country and only updating your family via Facebook. You aren't expected to stay near your parents and care for them. Your hometown is just the place where you grew up.

This is new for Jews in many ways and our communities haven't quite adapted. Jewish social activity in so many places is geared towards what feels like a desperate attempt to keep what little we have left in place. As someone coming in from the outside this baffles me because I see such a rich and incredible world of history, spirituality and diversity that I can't imagine how anyone could get bored. Compared to what I know of other religions, none of them compare to the depth Judaism has to offer.

That is all intellectual though. Many Jews sit around and talk about how we are losing our religious traditions or how cultural pluralism has reduced Judaism to a checkbox on a form, but those are just symptoms. The real concern is that Jews aren't going to shul. There is an interesting revelation to the High Holy Days and it's not the spirituality of the days themselves. Walk into any synagogue during this time and you will see a fully packed room. This is true everywhere I think, even in my very small town that normally sees 10 or 15 people at a service will have hundreds during the High Holy Days. There is nothing else like it and if your first trip is during this time, well, you might be disappointed after the fast.

Judaism is a way of life; it is not just a religion so in previous times the synagogue was a core of Jewish activity. People came and went all day doing various mitzvoth. As I understand it, Jews did not just show up during service hours and then leave, they came to pray whenever they could and only held to the time-bound mitzvot in a group. Having Jews at the synagogue wasn't an issue and everyone's children grew up there.

Today the synagogue is like a church in many places. The doors are only open for services and social events. We even have Sunday school which is actually the first day of the week as Shabbat has already passed. Everyone shows up at the same time and leaves at the same time. As a result, the only reason to go to the shul is for services or events. This means people can easily skip out.

The High Holy Days crowd gives you an idea of the population you really have versus the population that show up for services on a regular basis. It's depressing. But it also gives hope because all of those Jews can be persuaded one way or another eventually and that takes us back to the Chabad method of evangelism. Raising money, trying to get synagogue membership rates up and struggling to form a minion are all parts of the modern everyday Jewish religious experience. I do worry that Jewish kids today will grow up seeing all things Jewish as purely optional, but I guess that's really the job of Jewish adults today to make sure they see them as valuable enough to keep.

17

Jew is a Verb

I have learned that doing anything Jewish with other Jews magnifies the experience 10-fold. It really is as simple as singing together, having a discussion on a Jewish topic or studying together. Studying is something really unique and meaningful and I didn't expect it to be so. Studying for me has always been a private and quiet thing. I kind of expected my Jewish studying to be alone in a library.

About 45 minutes away is a Conservadox/Orthodox synagogue and they have daily minions and Torah/Talmud study classes. I attended one at the request of the rabbi there and I have to say that even with several Christians in the room, actually reading from the Talmud and discussing it was amazing. In Torah or Talmud study you pick a verse and then talk about it in connection to previous study experiences. You can spend an entire hour dissecting a sentence trying to puzzle out all of the various meanings and interpretations. Believe me there are multiple interpretations and every person in the room disagrees. It can be a little chaotic as people fight for their time to express why they disagree while others attempt to do the same thing, but in the end, it forces you to think about what you believe.

Discussing whether or not you can eat an egg laid on Shabbat causes you to reevaluate everything you think you know and believe about Judaism and G-d in general. Sometimes it's really easy to say that you believe something, especially when its vague, but when you are forced to apply that belief to a painfully specific topic it puts it into a new perspective.

Judaism is not a belief-based religion really. Everyone is expected to engage and understand. Saying you believe Jews should or should not follow a commandment for example can be viewed in massively different ways depending on the situation you are presented with. Nothing challenges you more than finding a perspective that conflicts with what you believe.

The challenge is not to give up when a conflict appears. You are not expected to be right all the time. If you smile with confidence to every scenario then clearly you are not thinking it through and you just want to win the argument. Allowing yourself to question the validity of what you believe makes that belief come alive. If you can wrestle it down again to a place where it works then you walk away stronger for it.

I love Judaism for this reason and my development has been stunted because I engage in this so infrequently.

Reading about what Rabbi this or that says on the topic and adopting it as your own is pointless. You have to be able to explain why it works and be willing to face the fact that it might not work at all. Even if it doesn't work you do not throw the entire thing away.

We live in a time where one must have firm opinions that never falter on every conceivable subject. If you find a subject that conflicts then you lose the argument and all credibility for future arguments. You become a "hypocrite" for agreeing to one scenario but not being sure about another. You must be 100% all the time. To avoid this intellectual absurdity people just choose what is already popular so they can merely point and use numbers of those who agree as evidence without needing to explain why.

Judaism does not allow this when you live it. I think many Orthodox are afraid to question because it looks like what Reform Judaism does and Reform Judaism is afraid to question because they appear to require an answer which sounds very Orthodox. Everything needs to fit nicely into its proper box. Being able to disagree with yourself in public in an honest way not only gives others the ability to do so as well but enhances the conversation to a new level. Are there yes and no answers? I think so, but we will never find out if we don't ask.

To be Jewish isn't just about doing Jewish things it is also about becoming a partner in Jewish thought and keeping the words of the Torah and Talmud alive by infusing them with your own personality and then sharing that with others. Jews can argue for eternity and never get an answer and by doing so Judaism never dies. It is only when Jews stop asking and merely repeat and paraphrase that Judaism loses its soul.

Going to services is so important and it's something I did not appreciate during my journey. I always thought of services as what you did after you became Jewish and felt comfortable in the role. I assumed you needed to learn Hebrew, know all the prayers/songs and actually be Jewish before any of it would make sense. I found that it doesn't work that way. How do you learn the prayers if you don't sing them every week?

I did not realize this until after I converted and I sat down for a Saturday service and had no idea what I was doing. There I was, sitting as a full Jew with full Jewish rights and responsibilities and I felt completely lost! I had always mimicked the prayers when we sang and followed along. I did not actually know the songs themselves. The moment everyone else stopped singing it was over! I needed to hear them in order to sing!

In all of my years studying and learning I never took time to get the basics down. Don't do that. Even though services can feel intimidating, especially in a smaller more intimate setting; I feel I have learned more from them than I did from a dozen books on the subject! Judaism can be readily absorbed intellectually, but to really experience it is completely different. Actually sitting and saying the prayers has such emotional and spiritual power that they cannot be overstated in importance.

Services are community events and often interactive. You are really joining together with your community and living a Jewish moment when you pray in services. When I first walked in the door and I experienced the crowd reading what sounded like drone nonsense to me, what I was missing was the nature of routine and the comfort it brings to a community. Call and respond services engage the community to affirm in public the principles which Judaism stands for. Even when it sounds like drone chanting it really is empowering to say those words together with a group of people.

Not all services are built like this of course, but for this style it can be viewed as boring if the spirit of the experience isn't realized. If you can really feel confident in the services and feel a sense of community and connection it will make the transition so much more meaningful. Services are usually the first thing a rabbi advises you to participate in before discussing conversion and this is why. When you participate with the community you get a strong feeling of what Jewish life for that community will be like.

When speaking with your rabbi make sure to talk about services and see if you can take home a service book. Usually Reform and Conservative synagogues will use a single book for the congregation to go by so it's easy to get used to. Mimicking the prayers is testing the waters, but you've got to be able to dive in at some point. Saying the Hebrew confidently and through practice allows you to feel the moment rather than worry about getting lost in the transliteration.

Something I did not prepare myself for was the participation expectation. In my synagogue members of the congregation actively participate in the production of the services themselves. People help take out the Torah, unwrap it and read passages. In a small congregation like mine, on Saturday Shabbat services, everyone is involved from reading the Torah portion to an Aliyah where you read a blessing. I am not great at public participation. I prefer to observe until I feel comfortable. Grabbing me and assigning me an activity to publicly perform when I am not prepared is horrifying to me. But Jewish participation in services is part of the deal.

Getting familiar with services for the synagogue you go to allows you to know what is expected and when it's time for you to do them yourself they won't feel so intimidating. I always worked in retail so my weekends were always full. I went to a Saturday service once and the rabbi asked me to open the curtain revealing the Torah scrolls. I was scared out of my mind because I had no idea how exactly one opened the curtains and I had to figure it out on the fly. It involved strings that if turned one way would pull the curtain open and then other would close it. It only took me two tries!

After I converted I went to a Saturday service and as I made a minion I got to see a different part of the service than I previously had before. I watched as individuals were called up, read something aloud in Hebrew and then kissed the Torah scroll with their tzitzit. It didn't take me long to realize the pattern and that I would be called up soon to do the same thing. I had never seen this blessing before nor been that close to the Torah scroll open. I was a newly minted Jew and felt an even more substantial need to perform well in public.

I admit I was annoyed with the rabbi because she knew I did not know what I was doing and yet she was calling me up anyways! Fortunately, I soon realized that no one else knew what they were doing either and the blessing was transliterated clearly so saying it wasn't as scary as I thought. Once I got past my public speaking anxiety (in a foreign language for a religious service) I enjoyed the experience of learning it. Had I been smarter and gone to more services before converting I would have known all about this!

The most surprising but important part of all this is that most people in the congregation probably feel just as lost as you do. Many Jews don't know the services or feel comfortable with Hebrew. I always assumed it was a club where all the members were experts at the secret handshake. I didn't realize that most were as unfamiliar as I was. The more you do the easier it comes to you and the less alien you'll feel.

There is one more part to living Jewishly that is implied but not as easy to exercise and that is what you do when no one else is looking. I have talked about this with eating kosher as an example, but there are also many other private Jewish requirements. No one asks you and there isn't an audit experience regarding them. Observant Jews assume you perform them if you are observant and non-observant Jews aren't too concerned. This part really is just between you and G-d.

I learned how to identify as a Jew and I learned how to socialize with other Jews. I developed an ethnicity and I explored spirituality and public celebration for years. I feel comfortable with much of that now. I always assumed the private stuff would happen on its own later. Jewish men, for example, pray every morning with tefillin and all Jews are supposed to pray before bed. Actually, Jews have three prayers every day and that does not include the many prayers about eating or other minor events that become elevated through spiritual recognition.

The more observant you become the more minutia you delve into and the more separate from social recognition it becomes. These are things done when no one is looking and no can judge your level of sincerity or correctness. This is motivated purely by personal will alone and there is no social reward or punishment involved. If you eat ham and cheese sandwiches at home every night, no other Jewish person will ever know. Devoting yourself to this path means deciding how you will live at home too.

Something that is important to keep in mind is that there is no "all or nothing" involved here. Every mitzvah you attempt counts each day and breaking one does not nullify the others. It can be tough getting past the feelings of being fake or a fraud that comes with the territory of adopting an entirely new ethnicity, but it significantly helps if you can feel confident in your own personal journey. Even though Judaism is a social religion, every Jew who performs even one mitzvah counts towards the whole.

18

Adventures of a Kippah

My Kippah
This is my kippah.
This kippah is green and brown.
To you it is a funny hat.
But this kippah has a secret;
It is a magic kippah.
It creates new worlds for you,
It spreads lies about mines;
It stays on my head all on its own.

I know you don't believe me,
But it's true.

This kippah is a meddlesome kippah.
It stays atop and watches you,
It knows what you are thinking.
This kippah is mine and it is not yours –
Please do not ask it to hide.
It would only shift to the top of my head
And defy you.[93]

My first Jewish challenge was, of course, my kippah. I got my first kippah from the synagogue gift shop back when I was 20 or so. It was black velvet with rainbow puffy glitter paint around the edge. Wearing a kippah for the first time is awkward. They don't really have an intuitive place to sit on your head really and everyone places them slightly differently. Over time mine has settled to where the center of the kippah lines up with my crown (where my hair swirls.) Sometimes guys have their kippah sitting directly on top of their head and I always think it looks funny. In any given situation where men and kippahs meet, you will likely see many tilted to the side as if they were expressing their inner gangsta, but really it has just slipped and they didn't notice.

Wearing my kippah in public for the first time was an adventure in itself. First I put it on my head and looked in the mirror and immediately felt ridiculous. Some are big enough to cover your head, but most are small and they sort of just stick out. I have red curly hair and my black kippah *really* stuck out. Kippahs made out of material also tend to not conform to the shape of your head as easily as woven ones do so it sort of perches there.

I decided to wear my kippah to the mall my first time out as I wanted to experience the most public exposure possible! The problem was I needed an excuse to wear it. I did not want to start wearing it every single day if I didn't like it so I felt that I needed to have specific reason, otherwise it might confuse people. Wearing it on Friday night made perfect sense even though I planned to go to the mall. I can still remember how self-conscious I was when I got out of the car and ventured towards the mall entrance. Remember, I live in a place where I still am the only one walking around with a kippah on in public so there was zero chance of blending in. My plan was to visit as many shops as possible and then go see a movie.

If memory serves, every single person in the mall instantly stopped what they were doing and stared at me in utter horror as I entered the building. Well, that is what it felt like anyways. I don't think anyone noticed. If they did not notice they didn't say anything to me. I walked every inch of that damn mall and didn't even get a confused look! But never fear, the experiment was not a waste.

Sitting down in the movie theater I felt vaguely annoyed that no one had even tried to discriminate against me and I had been there for hours! Contemplating the contrast between how obvious and loud I felt wearing my kippah with how no one seemed to notice I slowly became aware of giggles behind me. Squinting, I stopped thinking and listened and then a small piece of popcorn rolled down my head and into my lap. Then another piece tapped the back of my head and yet another floated by my head. I stiffened and felt my face turn red when I heard the girl a few seats behind me say to her boyfriend: *"Go get him! I hate that stupid little hat on his head! It looks stupid."*

I would like to point out that imagining conflict in fantasies where you are both brave and witty is one thing but actually realizing you might experience a conflict is completely different. Fortunately, the boyfriend told her no and to shut up and nothing else was said. That was my first and only negative experience with my kippah by the way.

At the time, however, it fueled my passion and made me three times as paranoid as I was previously. If you remember my earlier stories you can now draw a nice linear path from here to there. In the first several years I went back and forth with wearing my kippah. I kept the black one until I was 23 or 24 when I accidentally left it in a bag that I sadly lost.

I made up my mind at the time that I would wear it when working on Friday nights and Saturday mornings and during holidays (ie: Chanukah.) I would time sunset and pull my kippah out of my pocket and put it on. The next day at sunset I would take it off again. I wore it all week during Chanukah. I remember that each time I was absolutely thrilled.

If you are noticing that none of this has anything to do with the actual purpose of a kippah you are correct. This particular object was for me a symbol of rebellion and determination towards my new life decision. Wearing my kippah in public, at work or even at home made me feel as though I was taking a stand. My kippah became a costume in many ways and slowly grew more complicated as the expectations of others overshadowed my own desires and motivations. For example, once I dressed up as Zombie Jesus for Halloween and it was also a Friday night, so I wore my kippah. Tell me what kind of sense that makes.

At some point several years ago I decided to start wearing my kippah anytime I went outside. I don't really remember what sparked this but I just decided that if I was going to be serious about this I would need to take this on 100%. I put my kippah on, walked outside and never turned back. I have worn my kippah ever since with only one day as an exception. I was walking to work and my kippah blew off and landed in the road. A car promptly ran over it and splashed it into the gutter. Walking into the building you would have thought I was covered in blood the way people reacted with concern.

Today my kippah is just part of my wardrobe. Where I struggled before feeling as though I needed to bow my head every time I spoke to someone to make sure they saw it clearly, now I forget I am even wearing it. The whole point is to be a reminder that G-d is always watching. It is a sign of respect and a symbol of your devotion to the Mitzvot. Forgetting you are wearing it defeats the purpose a bit but it is a human flaw of mine. I sort of felt for a while that if I ever stopped wearing it, I would have to explain to every person who knows me and that would be too much effort. I feel a bit differently now though. More on that in a minute, right now I have more funny stories to tell you.

So, wearing a kippah in a place where it is unusual to do so does actually creates curiosity. I am sure you probably notice when a woman walks in with a hijab. Wearing a kippah directly signals to everyone around you that you are a Jew and for many of those people it also means you are a religious or observant Jew. Some people assume I am a rabbi. I seriously have had people approach me and call me "rabbi" and ask me Biblical questions. They just couldn't imagine a man wearing a kippah could be anything else.

Over the years, I have come to find it endlessly amusing how often other people ask me what exactly it is I have on my head. I can be going through a drive-thru, walking in a grocery store or working out and people will stop me, look at my head and then ask me what my little hat is. What I think is funny is that they know what it is because they usually follow up with *'Does that mean you are Jewish?'*

My absolutely favorite line is: *'Ok, don't be offended, but are you Jewish?'* Sometimes I want to react in horror and shout out *'How DARE you!'* Most people are just curious though. They have read about us in books, but to see one in real life? I do the same thing when I see a real-life nun. I mean, I don't stare at them or ask them personal questions because that is rude, but I get it.

People have lots of questions about my kippah. I have a few in different colors and once when I changed over to a new one someone asked me if I had just graduated to a higher level of Jew. You know, like I leveled up or something. I guess Catholics have a color-coded system that would make sense for that. I think Orthodox Jews sometimes all wear black kippahs, but as far as I know color and style choice are just fashion and have no significance. I can wear a SpongeBob SquarePants kippah if I want to.

Besides wanting to know what it is exactly, they are also endlessly fascinated by how I manage to keep it on my head. A friend of mine told me that Judaism must be the only true religion because there is no other explanation as to how the little hat stays on all day! It is just so funny to me how fascinated people are by this little hat.

You do need to know how to keep it on though. It is not an easy learning curve. You would think this is the easy part but it's not. Years ago, I prided myself on the fact that it just always stayed on, but as I began wearing it more often it did not stay so easy to maintain. You have to consider your hair length for one thing. When my hair is really short it sort of acts like Velcro and sticks to my head but as my hair grows this works less well. Some kippahs have clips built in but I could never really figure it out without scratching my head to pieces. I currently buy hair clips that snap in shades of gold, copper and brown. I don't like bobby pins. I did the side clip for a while where you put one clip on opposite sides but then I lost one and changed over to a single clip in the front.

None of this protects you from the wind however! I have just gotten used to walking through a windy parking lot with one hand holding onto my kippah. Driving with the windows down poses its own challenges too. With a single clip in the front you end up with the kippah flipping up and flailing about and if you clip both the front and the back, wind manages to get caught underneath it and you look like you have a miniature parachute on your head!

Rain and snow require an umbrella and having a wet kippah is like wearing wet jeans. If you wear a knitted kippah and it gets wet it will lose its nice skull-conforming shape and will never be the same again! This also goes for if you accidentally wash and dry it because it got caught in your shirt when you took it off or you left it in a pocket! It doesn't keep you warm in the winter but you notice it when it's really hot and sweaty out.

How do you ride a roller coaster? I don't know as I haven't ridden one since I started wearing mine all the time. Swimming is out of the question and working out is a bit complicated too. I tried lifting weights while wearing my kippah and it was a mess, not to mention it got caught on the machines anytime my head got in the way! I feel like it falls into the same category as glasses do. I need them to see but I don't work out or swim with them on.

There is no science to back this up but I swear the hair underneath it grows more slowly. Your head does get itchy during the day and you will find yourself checking the mirror to make sure it is still nicely centered. I can feel when my kippah is not in the right place and I can now put it on without the assistance of a mirror. It does make you consider other things like wearing normal hats. I used to wear a variety of other hats and now that feels extra awkward. Realistically as long as your head is covered you are good, the kippah is just a custom and is easily recognizable as being Jewish.

If you go through the metal detector some guards make you take it off while others just swipe it. Funny story, I once had to remove it in order to take a standardized test because they were afraid I could hide cheat sheets under it. It just adds a new level of consideration to your everyday life. I wasn't honestly prepared for all of that. Were there times I just wanted to take it off and forget it? Yes. But fortunately going through those challenging experiences better prepared me for my everyday life today so I appreciate it.

I promised you funny stories and I haven't forgotten. For years, I would venture out on my own and report back what I experienced and people would squint and humor me but I don't think they believed me. People didn't really ask me these things, did they? As I grew more comfortable with it myself I gradually became less self-conscious about it in public. Whenever someone would flag me down or abruptly point out my kippah it would rattle me a bit because I honestly wasn't prepared for it.

I was once eating with a friend when the restaurant began filling with smoke. Apparently, the smoke fan in the back malfunctioned and was blowing it into the dining room. As we all began making our way through the crowd of panicked people leaving, I was suddenly grabbed by the arm by a woman sitting at her table. *"Excuse me Sir! Are you Jewish?"* she called out with her hand wrapped around my arm with an unsettling grip. Remember, the room was now filled with smoke and we were trying to leave among a crowd of others when she did this. My friend looked back a bit horrified but didn't know what to do. I did what I always do which is smile politely, say Yes and then break eye contact and hope they go away. She didn't.

"Are you going to your temple right now? Oh! Please pray for my many children! We talked about the Jewish people at church and I just love the Jewish people!" Trying very hard not to be rude to this woman I nodded and tried to escape barely pulling from her reach as she cried out the names of her many children and continued to beg me to pray for them. My friend thought that was the most absurd thing she had ever seen and couldn't imagine how on Earth a person would think that was a reasonable thing to do. Little did she know it was fairly normal for me.

Another time she and I were eating at a Chinese restaurant when the waitress pointed at my head and asked me what my little hat was. She giggled and poked it and then she took it off my head. She just reached out and plucked it right off and looked it over. My friend displayed that same horrified face and never having someone actually grab my kippah before I tried to remain polite but I was unsettled. The waitress then placed my kippah on my friend's head and began giggling with absolute delight. She then frolicked away and joined several other staff and they pointed at us and laughed and laughed.

People don't really understand honestly. I once did not have my kippah clipped on and I quickly looked down as something fell and my kippah fell to the floor. The person speaking to me froze in terror and nearly knocked me over to grab it off the floor and began frantically brushing it off and apologizing over and over. With an eyebrow raised I took it back and placed it back on my head without concern. She was almost in tears with worry that I had just somehow been, I don't know, excommunicated or something. It is not a holy object at all and it is largely symbolic. There is a joke about two boys who are brothers going into the synagogue and they are both called up during services but one forgets his yarmulke. The mother realizes this and motions for the other boy to cover his brother's head with his hand and the boy responds loudly: *"What am I? My brother's kippah?"*

Many Jewish men only wear their kippah when they walk into a synagogue or when they eat Shabbat dinner. Others wear it continuously, even when they sleep. Many Conservative and Reform women wear one with the same variety of pattern as the men do. The purpose honestly is very personal and it does not need to be a requirement. I personally think wearing a kippah is a wonderful way to go through your day. Even when you forget for a time that you are wearing it, someone will come by and remind you. When you remember it's there you suddenly remember to behave too. Non-Jews can see you and might associate what you do with all Jews later. You will be the *Jewish one* when they see you.

I joke that I used to be a white guy because of this. Sure, my race is the same and no one would confuse me physically with anything but a very pale red-headed white guy, but when they see my kippah I suddenly become a Jew. For reference, White Supremacists do not consider me 'white', noodle on that for a minute. Jews are different. People treat me very differently. This was more distinct when I did not wear my kippah every day. I was once working at a store during Christmas when a woman approached me and asked me to kindly get her several nativity scenes for her to examine more closely. While doing so she mused that she was grateful I was there that day because she stopped by the day before and there was a Jewish guy working and she felt too uncomfortable asking him to get her nativity scenes.

One Halloween at work I did not dress up and after about the fifth time being asked what my costume was I just took my kippah off and said, *'Look, I'm a white guy!'* It is hilarious how true this really is. A simple circle of cloth can determine how others see you entirely. But what matters more is how it forces you to see yourself.

My kippah is possibly the most defining aspect of my Jewish journey. I always felt I could control my Jewish destiny and identity with this little hat. Putting it on and wearing it in defiance of everybody felt empowering. It was the one thing I could really do to feel Jewish. In the end, though, it did not make me Jewish. Today when I put on my kippah it is not about making a statement or trying to call attention to diversity. I could take my kippah off and never wear it again in public and I would be just as Jewish. For me it is a symbol of who I chose to become and it helps me recognize that the decision is larger than just me.

I wear it to honor G-d with my words and my actions and it keeps me honest. I wear it to connect to the millions of Jews in the world who take this simple action every day and link themselves to the large group. I wear it because it is a part of me and my practice of faith.

Other items of Jewish identity and religious practice come into play as you find yourself more and more active in Jewish life. Like my kippah, I was fascinated by the Star of David as well. Jews often refer to this as a Magen David. The little star is worn in many of the same ways Christians wear crosses. I had trouble finding one at first though and when I did I felt I needed to combine it with a cross too so I could fully express my variety of religious experience. I remember a friend of mine warning me others would find it offensive. To this day, I get a little uneasy seeing someone combining the two symbols together and I understand what he meant.

I did wear a Star of David necklace for a long time but I did it in the same way I wore a kippah. I felt it was a statement I needed to make. I absolutely hate jewelry however so it did not remain part of my wardrobe. Jewish people do like to decorate themselves with this symbol. It can be found on just about every Jewish related item you can buy too. For me, I often feel a strong sense of comfort when I see one and I enjoy having them around. I just never got in the habit of wearing one myself.

Tzitzit is another Jewish item that has a lot of significance but I have not yet incorporated into my lifestyle. This is a very unique piece of clothing because it is an optional commandment but represents the whole of all of them. Tzitzit is a requirement to put fringes on the corners of a four-cornered garment. If you don't wear a four-cornered garment then you don't need to follow the mitzvah. You only wear it during the day because you need to be able to see the strings. The corners have a complex series of knotted strings which may or may not contain a blue string depending on who is wearing it.

The fascinating part of Tzitzit is that they represent a reminder to do all of the commandments. The strings and knots add up to 613 somehow and you see the fringes during the day and remember to perform mitzvot. The garment itself is a little awkward because it is basically a poncho that doesn't cover your arms. If you took a tank top and cut the sides all the way to just under your arms you'd get the idea. They are made in a variety of ways and need to be Kosher and properly cared for. They are part of an Orthodox Jew's everyday wardrobe.

I was really curious about these a few years ago and so I bought some online. The material was similar to T-shirts in feel and weight but it felt awkward under clothes for me. I'm sure it would be like getting used to my kippah over time. The shirt gets tucked in but the strings need to be visible. Because of this some Jews have simply put the strings on key-chains and attach them to their belt loops although this is not considered kosher for the commandment.

When I wore them, people did notice more than I expected and I got a lot of questions from people who thought I had upgraded in Judaism again. This is one of those things that if you start you have to keep going with or people will start to get concerned. I found them awkward as they kept getting snagged on everything. I was aware of them all of the time but not for the reasons intended. My big issue, though, was washing it. I had no idea what I was doing and I washed them with my normal clothes. The fringes became tangled and broken and I never could fix them.

Wearing Tzitzit was also a controversial thing in my community as well. I am not sure if it was because I was not yet Jewish or if it was just too much for them, but I got a lot of negative feedback. I was even directly told to take them off. I suppose if I wore them more often they would get used to it. I feel like this particular item requires both a deeper understanding of daily Jewish practice and a devotion to consistent practice. I am just not there yet. I don't think I would recommend them to a new person though as they are fairly involved and represent a significant level of Jewish observance. If you think eating a cheeseburger while wearing kippah sends the wrong message, try doing it with tzitzit on!

Oddly the more common version you might see is the tallit. This is the wide scarf men and women wear in synagogues on Saturday mornings. They can be any color and design as long as they have the fringes at the bottom. If you go into a synagogue you are likely to see a wall of folded pieces of white fabric with blue and silver embroidery on them. These are the public use tallit. Many Jewish people have their own. Traditionally this, like tzitzit, is a male thing but women in Reform and Conservative congregations wear them too.

For me this felt like a line I should not cross. The Tallit is significant and is worn for prayer. You must be

Jewish to wear it and I always felt it was something I needed to wait for. I went to a Yom Kippur service once and had one placed on my shoulders and so I awkwardly kept it on even though I felt like I was seriously being sacrilegious doing so and another time when I went to a Saturday morning service someone tossed one on me. But for me I just would not wear one until I converted. When I did convert, I did actually wear one for my welcoming ceremony and then the following Saturday morning services. It felt like a final joyous acceptance for me to put it on and really feel as though I belonged. It has religious meaning and depth because its purpose is so closely connected to prayer.

They are itchy, however, and there is no way around it. I am told that if you have your own and use it all the time the fabric softens, but the public use ones are itchy. The embroidery is that sharp plastic material and you just sit there trying not to scratch the whole time. They are a little unwieldy too. They are wide and it takes some fussing to get each side to be bunched up enough to allow arm movement. I sat on the fringes the first Saturday morning and when I had to stand up I just about fell over as my neck was yanked downwards.

As I will talk about in the next chapter, the object itself has no power or influence itself. You wear it to pray and to be wrapped in the wonder of G-d and really embrace the prayers. Wearing it like a costume helps you begin to understand what it feels like to be Jewish but you have to know what that means first.

Another significant and mysterious Jewish object is tefillin. Tefillin is the leather strap you see wrapped around a Jewish man's arm and the little box on his forehead. I have worn tefillin once and that was a week or so before my conversion. This item is a one of a kind thing you own and embrace for your entire life. They are expensive but you only ever need one. The wrapping is done in the morning during prayers and is very personal. Jewish men (and some women) wrap tefillin in a morning minyan for prayer but it is often something done privately.

At some point, you have to decide how you will truly practice Judaism and that means waking up early and saying prayers every day. It is a significant commitment to do this, but it becomes a very holy and meaningful experience that makes each day special. This is a level of observance I have not gotten close to yet.

What about the black hat or that round fuzzy hat or the long black jacket? When people think of a Jewish man they typically have a visual in their head that involves a long beard, curly side-locks and a black hat. You probably also see a standard set of dress pants, white shirt and a long black coat. This is actually more of a Chassidic thing which is a sect of Orthodox Judaism. They do wear a long coat because traditionally long coats were a sign of respect. Jewish tradition is all about showing respect for G-d in all things and never slumming around. It is mostly a custom for a particular group of Jewish people and connects them together in dress.

When I began my journey, I was very focused on *looking* Jewish. Today I realize that you can wear all of objects together at once and it doesn't mean a thing if you don't know how to use them. Each has a purpose and a spiritual significance and each plays a role in your day to day life. At some point, you just stop dressing like a Jew and begin being a Jew.

19

People Hate Jews?

Anti-Semitism is something every Jewish person has to understand. Unfortunately, it's far more difficult to grasp than one would think. People often place anti-Semitism in the same group as racism or homophobia and it's something we obviously do not accept in a civil society. The problem is that anti-Semitism goes far deeper than any other kind of hatred. Racism can be the assumption of superiority or inferiority based solely on skin color. Homophobia can be the fear of social change or feelings that don't make sense but seem unnatural etc. Anti-Semitism is a deeply held belief that Jews cause the world's problems and are the result of evil.

It's strange to think like that. Today most Christians don't feel like Jews are evil, but in the past they believed Jews not only rejected their savior but murdered him. Centuries of Jewish massacres happened because of that singular perceived offense. Muslims trace the split back to Abraham's sons Isaac and Ishmael where Judaism follows Isaac and Muslims follow Ishmael.[94] Both contain scripture strongly attacking the Jews and both have caused tremendous persecution for Jews over the centuries. Even with our politically correct rose-colored glasses on we can see ongoing and explicit Jew-hatred across the Muslim world whereas the Western world expresses it in new and sometimes difficult to understand ways. Becoming a Jew is, in part, taking off those glasses and viewing the world as it is versus how you would like it to be.

One of the confusing parts of reading books about conversion to Judaism was the often-mentioned warning label that becoming Jewish could be dangerous. Part of the agreement you make when you convert is to vow to stand with the Jewish people when they are attacked or persecuted. People, including many Jews, will tilt their head to the side and ask you why in the world you would choose to become Jewish as though it's a ridiculous concept. I remember believing that all of this was just nonsense.

In my daily life, I never saw anyone attacking Jews, discriminating against Jews or encouraging either of the two. When I began to identify as Jewish no one ever reacted in horror or attempted to beat me up. I was never chased out of a store or glared at until I left myself. People either completely ignored it or they had lots of curious questions. It wasn't until the experience at my college I told you about earlier that I experienced anti-Semitism in any real form.

Older Jews have a different experience going back to when they were openly discriminated in the work place or denied entry into various colleges or hotels. Obviously, there are many who witnessed the Holocaust or whose parents did. When they speak about anti-Semitism you can see in their eyes how differently they view it than we do. The thing is that in the US you are probably not going to experience anything negative specifically for being Jewish in any modern way. It doesn't mean anti-Semitism is gone however. It took me a long time to be able to recognize it myself. I used to think people were just being overly paranoid or sensitive. I have learned a lot.

For me I see anti-Semitism really falling into three categories: Blatant hatred, Ignorance and Israel. To begin with, yes, there are neo-Nazis in the US and unfortunately throughout Europe, mostly ranting online. Sometimes they hold rallies and where I live there is a man with a Hitler tattoo on his arm and a swastika on the back of his neck who has a wife and children and at least one other guy with various Nazi imagery on his body. I saw them once at Wal-Mart and they chose to use the opposite side of the doors. The man with a Hitler tattoo was once beaten and no one would help him along the highway. I worked as a night guard at a hotel and he staggered in bleeding. I called 911 and helped him until they got there. I wasn't wearing my kippah that night.

Outside of Muslim protestors with swastikas on signs and radical clerics calling for the death of Jews, you really don't see a loud blatant anti-Semitism that often.

Ignorance seems to be more common and it falls into a grey area where it's not always malicious but it definitely can be used to make the experience of a Jew difficult. Ignorance is really just stereotypes about Jews, inappropriate jokes or skewed expectations. For example, it never ceases to amaze me how often people think jokes about Jews and ovens are funny.

We live in a highly individualized world where group affiliation, especially with regards to religion, is often fluid. Being black, gay or Christian does not necessarily connect you to all black people, gays or Christians. Our society is very focused on preventing the establishment of a standard towards members of a group by that group alone or by the individual alone.

One cannot demand that all of one kind of people are alike. The very idea that we have *kinds* of people at all is disturbing to many. Jews are not individually able to be separated from Jews as a *people*. The Jewish people is a concept unbroken across time or land without distinction to the various levels of observance. An atheist Jew in New York, a secular cultural Jew in Russia or an Ultra-Orthodox Jew in Israel are all in the exact same category.

Jews have an incredible diversity that makes it even harder to grasp since we span the globe and can be found in nearly every culture on Earth. Regardless of our race, or observance or our ancestry we are Jews. People do not always understand that. It is quite difficult to seamlessly blend this into our everyday lives as well since we are so used to being individuals. For me it was mindboggling to grasp that I was truly joining a people rather than just adopting a new a religion.

Religion is often viewed as part of a person's life which is dependent upon that person's experiences and life choices. At any time that religion may become more or less relevant or can be replaced or nullified. You can't do that with Judaism. In my experience, no one understands that. I recently saw an article focused on a Modern Orthodox political leader[95] who had to decide if he would break Shabbat or vote on an important issue. The comments section lit up with condemnation as to what was most important. People demanded that the issue itself was more important than some silly religious ritual. Others opined how Jews pick and choose which rituals are significant while ignoring others. I saw several sweeping declarations that since that particular commenter knew Jewish people who did not follow certain rules no other Jew could reasonably have credibility in their need to follow those same rules.

These were people with whom I agreed with politically and who never show any negativity towards Jews yet with the ignorance of our religious and social structures it easily became hostile. This is certainly not contained to one side or the other. Liberal and conservative non-Jews often express annoyance towards Jewish religious standards in this same way.

Another area for this expression is specifically between Christian and Jewish religious comparison. In the above example, several people decided that since Jesus nullified the old laws this act of religious devotion was pointless. Others quoted from Christian scripture to prove the same point. After reading several of these I realized that the main area of contention was that they believed Jews chose when to make their religion important and when to ignore it and expected everyone else to respect that decision. The commandments were seen as unnecessary and manmade and they were sure that G-d never meant for any of it.

Whenever religious discussion comes up I often see a clear misunderstanding of the Talmud's role in Jewish religious practice, the idea of observance at all or the role of Rabbinical decision making. Christians sometimes express disapproval of the idea that a Rabbinic court could determine whether something follows G-d's laws or not. Purists who say every word in the Bible is exactly intact as it is are offended by interpretation and completely dismiss the Talmud altogether. In the end, religious discussion turns into an argument with a flawed premise. Christians believe in one concept of the Bible and Jews an entirely different one.

A great example of this would be the never-ending demand that the Bible does-too condone slavery. If one reads Leviticus it clearly talks about slaves and you cannot deny it! An in-depth discussion through the Oral Torah and Rabbinical discussions shows you that slavery as we know it is nowhere near what is being discussed, yet to include that argument immediately calls upon dismissal.[96] While this isn't a direct hatred of Jews, it is hostility towards our history, religious practice and the foundation of our very understanding of G-d's word.

Ignorance of what is really going on with the added layers of stereotypes creates an environment where a Jewish person is expected to defend themselves against whatever accusation is being thrown at them. While we do not necessarily find ourselves being accused of using the blood of Christian children for our matzah, we are often accused of dismantling the Bible to fit whatever view we wish based on rabbinic ruling.

When someone rolls their eyes at our silly rituals they are in fact dismissing us as a whole even if they don't mean to. Unlike other religions, there really is no separation between Jewish religious ideas and the Jewish people. Even those who are completely unobservant are affected when non-Jews decide they don't like something we do or believe. This is difficult because we are encouraged to question things we do not understand. I have no problem stating that I do not find the same religious value in Jesus or

Muhammad as Christians or Muslims do and I don't think that says anything negative about either group or any individual within that group. But I know that when someone so strongly questions why I need to not eat ham or gets annoyed with me wanting to observe Shabbat, it affects me as a person and not just my religion. It is like looking at me and telling me how disgusting it is that I need to eat. Jewish law and the Jewish people are one in the same and even without realizing it; the social acceptance of hostility towards Jewish law is anti-Semitism.

The most controversial area of anti-Semitism, especially in modern day, is Israel. Nothing clearly defines how people view Jews as a whole more than how they view Israel. That sentence alone is enough to start a very heated argument. This issue divides Jews like almost nothing else and is the most intellectually challenging experience to undertake. How is it that a political or social disagreement over Israel could impact all Jews?

Many Jews will demand that criticism of Israel or anti-Israel sentiment has nothing to do with Jews at all. To say that anti-Israel views are anti-Semitic will get you a squinted look from non-Jews and sometimes even an argument. People have managed to separate the two in their minds and are comfortable with Jews as people but extremely hostile towards Israel. I do not think that a negative view of Israel directly connects to Jew-hatred but I do think that people who hate Israel do not always realize what they are doing to the Jewish people.

Before the modern state of Israel, Jews were completely dependent on the good nature of the peoples they resided with. As stated before, Jews were never members of any country. The state of Israel allowed Jews to have a single place in all the world where they could be safe as Jews and not need the permission of others to stay that way. No one could come in and tell them to get out of their own country. To this day, Israel remains the safest place for Jews in the world with the US coming in second.

Certainly, Israel today is not the Biblical representation. It is a democracy without a temple or a King, but it is a place for Jews that no one else should be able to touch. The world is not moving towards sovereign land any longer though and with our world becoming more open and the walls of countries falling it has been difficult to maintain this idea. People even go so far as to claim it is racist for Israel to be a *Jewish* state as no country should have such a specific designation.

Furthermore, the cries have not been for the safe integration of Jews into the rest of the world or a promise that we will never again be kicked out, rounded up or massacred. The only demand has been to take away the land from the Jewish people. Look at a map of the Middle East and it becomes absurd that Arabs need to also occupy that tiny strip of land along the ocean. Muslim and Arab countries are vast and there is no logical reason for one population that is no different at all from the other Muslim populations in the area to require a piece of Israel too.

But logic doesn't seem to be involved with this discussion. Rabbis everywhere will insist that the never-ending peace process between Israel and the Palestinians will one day ensure a safe place for Jews. Many Jewish organizations focus on the mythical oppression of Palestinians more than they care that this is the only place on Earth they will ever be safe. As stated previously, it just is impossible to be neutral on this issue.

When you see anti-Israel propaganda, rallies or messages they look exactly like they did back when they were anti-Jewish. There is no difference. Before Jews kidnapped children and drank their blood, now Israel murders children on the streets. It's the same lie told again. When I read anti-Israel articles, books or see videos I can feel the anti-Semitism that older Jews describe decades ago. Where I cannot understand it today in terms of myself as an individual Jew in my society, I can understand it as a collective Jew with the state of Israel.

One final observation that hits closer to home for me personally. As a politically interested person I am often on the forefront of controversial social movements and events. I am on the political Right while most Jews are on the political Left. Since President Trump was elected the media

has been aflame with r
Supremacist activity
me how I deal with
also on the Right.

Without
answer is that t
a singular identity.
can go very far to the edge
would disagree, I do not see the sam
or other manifestations of anti-Semitism on
college professors and anti-Israel demonstrators.
told, the former merely say terrible things online while the
latter act out in public, often utilizing violence and intimidation.

I tend to care more about action than I do words and it is easy to ignore those who seem to enjoy the fantasy of a Jewish World Order in which Jews control everything in their lives. Whether it is a Neo-Nazi using 'Jew' as a slur or a Pro-Palestinian advocate calling me a 'Zionist' they mean the same thing. Anti-Semitism is not bound by political ideology.

20

Run Rabbi, Run

As previously mentioned, there was that curious rabbi whom I mentioned seemed very intent on ignoring me all these years. I couldn't leave you hanging with just that. There is more. I'm not bitter. As I mentioned, upon my first meeting the rabbi dismissed me without even so much as a half-interested nod to my, likely, over-enthusiastic declaration that I wished to become Jewish. I also mentioned that for some time after, *coughs* seven years *coughs*, he continued this policy. You might be asking yourself why. He never really brought it up. I did finally sit down with him at the seven-year mark to discuss conversion and he was very supportive but we never went any farther. The meeting next week got canceled and then something came up and so on.

I admit I spent the last decade just thinking he didn't like me. I don't know why he didn't like me. Everyone likes me. But as I evolved through this process he was just always missing from it. I even took a class called *Judaism 101* with him as my professor. I think I missed about half of it as I did most of my classes that semester for medical reasons. Nevertheless, I think that it displays a nice example of what might have happened with this unique person in my Jewish life.

I had always looked to him to give me permission and to show me enthusiasm for my choice. I felt like he, out of everyone, needed to be behind me in this, otherwise it would never really work. I wanted him to be my rabbi. But in his defense, I never really gave him a lot to go on.

I think that after my first meeting and then the subsequent ones that I felt it was his turn to reach out to me. I wanted him to recognize me for my Jewish behavior in real life and I wanted him to point to me as an example of someone trying to really embrace Judaism. I always interpreted his ambivalence to mean he was disinterested or even worse, disapproving. I think he was a little disapproving actually. I did, after all, spend half a decade strutting around his town wearing my Jew costume and demanding equal Jewish treatment. I never went to services or participated in Jewish activities and the only time he ever saw me was when I appeared to be playing the 'who's more Jewish' game by wearing my kippah. I should have picked up on the clues.

His wife mentioned several times with a slight squint of her eyes: *'So I understand you are doing Jewish things…'* and then would advise me to go to services or talk to her husband. I wanted to say back *'I tried lady but he won't* *answer the %$^&! phone!'* I also think that my youth had something to do with it. I was 19 when I first approached him and truth be told I was a drastically different person then. I have come to understand that I did not do all of this in a bubble like I imagined. I spent so many years making my own choices and fighting my own battles about becoming Jewish that I never took into consideration that other people, let alone other Jews, could see me. As has been politely inferred, some were a bit curious about the goy running around with a yarmulke on his head all these years.

I never really waited to ask them first if I could join their community. I just put the little hat on and went with it. I think that looking back my biggest mistake that I would correct now is that I wanted it too quickly and too badly. I didn't know what I was asking for and I didn't know who it was I was asking to become partners with. I didn't know these people and yet I decided I was one of them? Just like that?

The conversion books did not talk much about the other Jews. They did not bring up the emotional impact or the sociological ripple effect diving in would cause. These people grew up in a small community together, relying on one another because of this label. It hasn't always been a wonderful multi-cultural world in which diversity was appreciated. Many of these Jews chose to keep their Judaism inside the synagogue because that was the only place it was safe. It would be as if you came home to a family dinner to find a complete stranger smiling up at you and calling you brother. When you asked your parents, they would just say *'I don't know, he just walked in and sat down.'*

To make it worse my overzealous approach to Jewish expression was not exclusive to my own experience. They experienced the effects that I caused by my actions. By forcing Judaism into so many public places where it did not normally live I forced actual Jews to become more visible than they may have liked. By my actions, I caused them to experience questions and strange looks. They had to explain on my behalf when some mutual acquaintance puzzled about what it was exactly I was doing out there.

I crashed the party and expected to be welcomed with open arms. I never even knocked on the door, I just walked in. The arrogance of the convert is to believe they deserve to be Jewish. Jews never asked for the lives they live and even though it can be wonderful and beautiful it is also difficult and sometimes dangerous. I might have made it just that more difficult and dangerous without even intending to.

All in all, I am grateful that this first rabbi did not welcome me the way I had imagined. I am grateful for the decade of experience that taught me the difference between deciding on a new religion and becoming a Jew. I needed that time alone and I needed to be forced to find Jewish people and befriend them. I needed time to acclimate to what being Jewish really is. I needed that decade. I needed the rabbi to tell me no.

He was, gratefully, part of my Beit Din and I realized all I just said above in the span of a very small period of time. Sitting with him, my rabbi and a long time Jewish friend I saw myself through their eyes for a time. As I explained myself and answered questions I could see that the primary hesitation was that I just never came to services or engaged with the community on a regular basis. I now know it was never an issue of his liking me or his willingness to convert me, it was really me appearing randomly and announcing myself without merit. I did not experience what I needed to and they knew it. This is what is known as "wisdom" on their part.

Every now and then I will hear of a person coming in to ask about conversion and it always starts the same way:'*"...and I told them they should come to services...'* I wasn't so different or interesting; I just missed some important steps along the way.

Finding your rabbi is a struggle because you may only have one choice depending on where you are and if you are like me that might be difficult if you don't get on right away. Building a relationship with your rabbi is key to this process. I kept reading that concept over and over and I always thought it was just a nice concept. What I needed was someone to sign the papers. Any rabbi would do!

I spent years meeting a rabbi about 45 minutes away from me but because of work, illness and gas I never got to really experience a steady flow. I would have to cancel or holidays or vacations would come up and then another few months would go by and we would start again. It wasn't his fault as he was wonderful I just couldn't get in step with what I needed to do because of distance. I really felt this was incredibly defeating and other Jews never appreciated the conflict I was experiencing.

I think born Jews don't get what the big deal is with converting. You spend a year doing the classes and holidays and poof you're a Jew, why complain? Besides the incredibly difficult emotional work and life-altering challenges there is also the ability to do it. Sometimes it is just expected you will find a way. Well I found a way; it just took me a decade. I think every potential convert should wait a decade.

During this up and down period my local synagogue needed a new rabbi as ours was going to retire. I was actually going to be watching the process of selecting the person who could be my rabbi for the next 20 years or more. Selecting a rabbi is a big deal. We had several candidates and sadly they do not debate like Presidential ones do although I think it would be beneficial to the process. They came one by one and spoke to the congregation. There was a young Conservative rabbi who leaned more Orthodox, two Reform female rabbis and one male rabbi with a guitar.

I remember the first female rabbi as she was also a convert to Judaism and that piqued my curiosity. She did what I wanted to do but like 20 times more. I admit I really liked the young almost Orthodox one because I felt that we had previously had a Reform rabbi and now a change to the other side might be good for the congregation and would also allow me a more in-depth Jewish experience. When it was announced that our rabbi would be a woman there were many mixed reactions. People who didn't care that she was a woman were very concerned that she was a convert. She had an uphill battle all the way. I was no help. I was disappointed that we would be headed in an even more Reform path and I couldn't move 45 minutes away to go to the Conservadox synagogue like I wanted to.

I just decided to avoid the whole mess and I oddly found myself back to my original plan of doing Judaism on my own, except now with some friends. I totally discounted her based on her gender and Reform views. She is very light hearted and thoroughly enjoys the rainbow of experience that is available from many different sources. I frowned at the idea of having a spiritual leader who seemed to believe that 'if it feels good, do it.' We had an event and she was invited and slowly I found myself interacting with a little more. She was incredibly enjoyable in person but I couldn't get past what I saw as huge downsides to her position. I was also entering my 10th year of living as a Jew without any right to do so. I admit that I decided originally to ask her to convert me as a starter home idea. I figured I would get a basic Reform conversion out of the way to get me in the door and then I'd move up the ladder as I went. We will call this 'Jewish level 1.' I contacted her, asked her to meet with me and she said yes. Then everything changed.

Meeting with her felt a little like being a spy. I felt I would talk about things and see how she responded. I wanted to understand her, I have to admit, but I was also firmly held in my belief that liberal + reform = silly hallmark card goodness and I just wasn't interested. I heard she changed the "He" to "Him/Her" and that she insisted on female options in praying to G-d. I fully expected a complete lesson in how to love one another with rainbows and tie-dye blankets where we could eat whatever food we wanted and talk about G-d, whoever She might be.

I felt like the harm in Reform conversions is that new Jews are not prepared to really appreciate Jewish life and religious obligation. Hell, there is no religious obligation! If they convert and have children and their children learn the same things, then Judaism just becomes a social identity and rabbis get turned into challahs and you know how I feel about all that by now. If a potential convert really delves into Judaism however and appreciates the commandments then conversion just requires the basics of a mikvah, the prayers and the realization of limited recognition. The newly Jewish person will hopefully go on to live an observant life so no harm done.

I wasn't sure if she would be dismissive of my religious ideals or if she would try to dissuade me from taking them so seriously but I decided to just go with it and get my papers. I believed there were perspectives and things I could learn from her because she expressed a strong desire for study and had already engaged in multiple public study classes that involved lots of interested people.

I loved that the congregation was involved and doing Jewish things even if they weren't as observant as I would hope. My first meeting with her, however, shattered most of what I had built up about her in my head. Yes, she is liberal and yes, she loves Reform Judaism but not because it knocks out all those silly outdated rituals but because she feels it allows the individual to find their own place in Jewish life. She also had her concerns about me as well. Her limited interactions with me had put me squarely in the position of being probably what she imagined as a typical conservative Republican. I mean I helped organize an event by Glenn Beck[97] for goodness sake!

We both sort of realized that we didn't know anything about each other. She allowed me to be open and honest and she was the same with me back. We talked about so many things and I found that I could express my concerns and questions to her and she listened and provided her perspective and it allowed me to really think and feel what it was I wanted. I knew intellectually what I wanted but I never really had been given the permission to do it.

After my first meeting my motivation moved from wanting to get this conversion thing done with already to really wanting to know what this person could teach me about Judaism. She did too. I learned that as passionate as I am about Jewish life I cannot be so aggressive and expect others to appreciate it on the same level. Jewish is as Jewish does truly and it is better to be involved in a little way than to not be involved at all. Sometimes being too strict pushes people away. Ironically for me being too open makes me lose security in the guidance provided. Sometimes I like a firm yes or no. But I needed to evaluate my goals. If my goal is to be a part of this community then I have to find my Jewish experience here.

I still don't like the organ on Shabbat and I feel very uncomfortable using female Hebrew pronouns when praying to G-d. I do think that the commandments are valid and important and I do not like the idea of Jews tossing them aside, but I am comforted that this rabbi in this place isn't trying to do that. I believe she sees great depth and beauty in Judaism and in her enthusiasm to share that she is lighting sparks in people who may never have walked into the building otherwise.

I think she in particular opened the door for me to understanding and appreciating Judaism in a way I didn't know I could before. I knew Orthodox Judaism existed and I could read about their perspectives and practices, but I wasn't doing any of them. I deeply appreciated what they brought to the world and the Judaism they held so tightly. I must state that knowledge is useless if it is not used. Of all the things I know, Jewish life and practice are still things I am learning and probably will always be learning.

In the end of this process I felt deeply grateful that she was there for me and was so open. We spoke for hours about so many topics and every time she mentioned a Jewish concept I found layers I just did not know existed before. She inspires me. I feel she is *my* rabbi now. Even though I met her in the last year of my journey towards this goal, she redefined everything I believed I knew before and she gave me permission to continue searching deeper.

21

Skinny Dipping with The Rabbi

My original goal in writing this book was to write about my journey towards future conversion. I wanted people to see my mistakes and learn from my experiences and hopefully apply them to their own conversion process. I wrote the first paragraph without knowing when I would ever truly become Jewish. As time went on and I realized this was a reality, I began to evolve the message. Then I converted to Judaism and that just blew everything out of the water. I pulled up this file and I decided to complete it as a whole. Everything written before was relevant still. In fact, actually completing the journey allows it all make a bit more sense I think.

Actually, converting feels very much like getting married as I understand it from others. I have known people who lived together for years and then got married and described it as being incredibly different. I never understood why. Now I think I might. The day before I converted I felt Jewish; when I walked out of the mikvah I *was* Jewish. In my community, the necessary components to Jewish conversion are focused largely on how a potential convert engages with the congregation.

Oops.

Some Beit Dins are focused on Jewish knowledge and testing you on the intricate details of Jewish practice. Mine was all about my journey and what I learned. I sat with both rabbis and an elder in the congregation and they asked me why exactly I was doing this. Even with a decade behind me, *why* was still very important. We talked about my early years, my name change and my previous family. We talked about my goals and what kind of Jew I hoped to be. It took about an hour and then I left the room and they decided. Fortunately, they all said yes, otherwise it would have been awkward for all the people I already sent invitations to for my ceremony!

They gave me a beautiful document detailing my commitment to this decision and I signed in it both my English name and my Hebrew name. They all signed it as well. But I wasn't Jewish just yet. I still needed to go to into the mikvah. The mikvah is like a very small pool. It's deep enough to fully immerse oneself. There are larger ones for groups, but the mikvah I went to was meant for a single person. Essentially this is a holy place with significant meaning for the person who uses it. The general idea is of purification. Now this is not a bathtub, you have to be *very* clean before you enter it. It is designed to purify a Jewish person or to, I guess, create a Jewish person in the case of a convert.

The idea is that you go in clean and naked bringing nothing with you but yourself exactly as G-d created you and then when you emerge from the water you are now a Jew as if you were born one. You actually go under three times and you have to make sure your hair is completely under as well. I think you also lift up your feet, I did at least. Each time you come up you say a prayer in Hebrew. The first is to thank G-d for His instruction on immersion, the second is to thank G-d for bringing you to this point and the third is to thank G-d for making you a Jew.

This is a deeply spiritual experience and the physical act of immersing yourself, by your own will, is impactful to the decision process. Up until that moment you were reliant completely on other Jews and a rabbi to give you permission. In the mikvah it's all you.

Did I mention you are naked? Yeah. This was one of my concerns when I first read about this. I imagined having to walk into a swimming pool surrounded by the Jewish men in my community to do this. I don't know where I got that idea but it made sense in my mind. My baptism was like that minus the naked part. Fortunately, this is private with just your rabbi and she couldn't see me. The mikvah was in a small room with a shower to the side and a door. After you got into the water you called the rabbi in and she stood outside the pool. So technically I was naked in the same room as my rabbi (thus the title of this chapter.)

I was nervous about the dunking part too. I don't dunk well. I have always been a hold-my-nose type when I go under water but I understand this isn't polite. I only experienced the water-up-my-nose panic once but I soldiered through. I struggle with experiencing things in the moment most of the time. I tend to think about how I should be feeling this or that and by the time I decide what it is I should be feeling it's all over. This was true here too. But I think having my rabbi there reading to me helped me stay focused on the experience itself.

Was it spiritual? Yes. Did I feel a magic glow or the touch of G-d or anything? No. When you are a Christian and you get baptized it's assumed you have a dove moment. You know, where a dove lands on you or something and you have a significant otherworldly angels-singing type of experience. Judaism is all about doing even if you don't fully understand why and appreciating that G-d knows best. I was naked in a pool of warm water trying to keep my hair out of my face and not choke to death while saying Hebrew; spiritual yes, magical no.

There was a brief time though when she left and I stayed in the water a bit longer and I realized that even without a sudden burst of supernatural euphoria I had just completed something I believed might be impossible for the entirety of my adult life. As I got out of the water and dried off it did hit me that it was *finished*. I did it. I truly did it. When I walked out to greet my rabbi and to go home I realized that my life did just change dramatically even if I wasn't fully aware of the details of how just yet.

The day after my mikvah I had my public welcoming ceremony. This was to happen during Friday night Shabbat services and its purpose was to officially introduce me to the congregation and for them to officially welcome me. I knew about this two weeks in advance so I had already treated it like a wedding. I invited people and prepared a speech and planned beautiful pictures and I nervously anticipated what I expected to be a defining moment in my life.

I was close. The evening of I got to have Shabbat dinner with my Jewish family. It was my first Shabbat as a Jew and even though they had always treated me as though I already was one, there was an excitement and bounce in the way they handled dinner. Praying, washing, eating the challah, all of it felt a bit more real. The service itself was very nice but I admit I was terrified of forgetting everything I planned to say in my head. I had been going over this for two weeks and every draft seemed insightful and humorous or deeply meaningful in my head as I fell asleep but would then seem a bit silly when I woke up.

I was still composing it in between responsive readings and prayers. The moment was planned to be after the Torah reading so I could hold the Torah and say the Shema. It was also warm in the room and I am a sweater. I'm genetically Irish and this heat nonsense just does not work with my biology. I need it to be around 68 degrees to be comfortable. I didn't want to be standing in front of my community looking like a standup comedian who wasn't doing as well as he hoped.

Fortunately, my rabbi is incredibly easy going and so when she did finally call me up I felt safe. I wore a tallit and amazingly said the prayer for it with articulation that surprised me. I held the Torah and looked into the crowd and I felt that sense of pride and embarrassing achievement many kids take for granted when they are publicly celebrated which I did not experience much with my own family. Growing up my public achievements did not involve me looking out into the crowd to see the proud faces of my family. I did experience that moment deeply. The rabbi was speaking and she sort of faded away and everything did go into slow motion and I could see true joy in the faces of the people looking back at me. That was my moment.

I was given a paper with a small script to say to the congregation and then I had the opportunity to say a few words myself. This is how it went:

I am a Jew because my faith demands of me no abdication of the mind.
I am a Jew because my faith requires of me all the devotion of my heart.
I am a Jew because in every place where suffering weeps, I weep.
I am a Jew because at every time when despair creis out, I hope.
I am a jew because the word of the people Israel is the oldest and the newest.
I am a Jew because the promise of Israel is the universal promise.
I am a Jew because, for Israel, the world is not completed; we are completing it.
I am a Jew because, for Israel, humanity is not created; we are creating it.
I am a Jew because Israel places humanity and its unity above the nations and above Israel itself.
I am a Jew because, above humanity, image of the divine Unity, Israel places the unity which is divine.

Ten years ago, I came here with the ambitious decision to become a Jew. I had no idea what I was getting myself into. I did not anticipate the depth, the culture, the incredible diversity. I did not expect to make such dear friends to be cared for; to be loved. I did not expect that.

You can say the prayers, sing the songs, wear a kippah and feel Jewish but you cannot decide to become a

> *Jew. You cannot make it happen. You are only a Jew if other Jews say you are. Your rabbi and your community, they must believe in you.*
>
> *I am asked why I would choose to become Jewish. Just look at the wisdom and history of our former rabbi, the joy, color and exuberance of our new rabbi. Look to the beauty and depth of our Torah. Shabbat dinners, Yiddish choir, celebrating Israel, signing and prayer together. It's you.*
>
> *You all are Judaism. You are the Judaism I know. You are the reason I am Jewish and I cannot express my gratitude for that.*

That is what I felt in my heart in that moment standing there talking to the people I worked so hard to be a part of. When they said: *"We rejoice to welcome into our midst one who willingly and devotedly helps replenish the ranks of our people. As you have chosen to link your fate and life with ours, so too do we accept you forever as one of us and pledge our support of you as a member of our congregation and as a member of the Jewish people."* I felt that acceptance and genuine joy I had longed for. This was so deeply significant for me to feel a part of this community that I honestly cannot express it. It defined my life from that moment on. All I had worked for finally made sense.

Can yo…

when I mused tha… get? I was wrong. Is the conv… to become a Jew? There is no longer an…

It is different now. I know it doesn't mak… any other religious context, but it is different now. I admit it is a bit awkward for people who have known me for at least 7 or 8 years to smile broadly and say *"Welcome!"* I have noticed a shift in the body language and the way I am approached even just a day later. The following Saturday morning I went to services and when I grabbed a tallit I didn't hesitate or look to the side to make sure no one frowned. I sat down and picked up the prayer I walked in the middle of and it was as if I had always been there. Suddenly it seemed so natural. There was no hesitation for me and no one even blinked. I am now just another average Jew.

Internally I noticed how I see things changed too. Always before I battled between an attitude of *'I don't care,*

want to offend anyone...' whenever I
would consistently preface whatever
Jewish yet' too and I would feel a small
perience anything fully. If I prayed too
commented on the Torah portion with too
dence I worried other Jews would be offended.
I don't have to worry about any of that. Well at
ot here or with Conservative/Reform Jews anyways.

I can say the prayers as though they are mine
cause they are mine. I can own Judaism as a part of myself and contribute without apology or hesitation now. I am one of the people in the room who can open the ark, hold the Torah, say a blessing or do anything Jewish. I count in a minion!

All in Judaism is now mine to explore. I am no longer visiting and trying things on respectively. I am now a Jew. That is significant to me not only in how others view me but in how I view myself. Jewish authenticity is a continuous weight on the shoulders of every Jewish hopeful, but now that is gone. I do wonder a bit how I will interact with more Orthodox Jews but I suppose I now have the authority to defend my Jewishness if need be. But since I don't plan to marry any of their daughters or enter their rabbinic schools I suppose it isn't something that will come up. As far as they know I am a Reform Jew.

Always before I would sit and repeat the prayers in services in large part to show I could participate and I hoped that my growing comfort and articulation would be a sign of my serious devotion. No one ever noticed. Now when I say a prayer I want to know it, own it, feel it and truly *say* it. I realized so much of the prayers I know are only from mimicking them so long that I can repeat them like a song. Now I want them to be my prayers to G-d. When I read passages, I want to understand them. I want to know what Hebrew is in a deep and personal way. When I put on a tallit or my yarmulke I want to know why and never take it for granted. It's not about proving myself any longer. Now I get to be it.

My congregation was incredibly kind enough to make me a member for free for a whole year! I am a member of my congregation now. I can vote and everything! But it also means I can participate. I can become an important part of my community here and help move us all forward. I am able to influence things and my voice will hopefully benefit my congregation. My actions truly will impact everyone there and theirs will impact mine as well. I already asked my rabbi to teach me the services so that I can jump in and lead if needed.

Some converts leave the mikvah or their welcoming ceremony and then never come back again except on Yom Kippur, but I plan to get on everyone's nerves as much as I possibly can. Having a genuine community is deeply significant to me. I don't know if they really thought this through when they decided to let me in. I used to think of

Jewish activities as ways to add another merit badge to my belt and prove my worthiness. Now there is an entire world open for me to explore. I believe this is the single most important thing I want you to walk away with: Converting to Judaism is just the beginning.

23

Advice

I know I said I wasn't going to try and tell you how to convert or all the details, but there are some things I hope you come away with. I figured some things out a bit later than I should have and I'd prefer you did not make the same mistakes.

Go to services. Seriously. When you first approach a rabbi about conversion you will be asked to come to services. This is not dismissal as much as it is an honest introduction. Hopefully you have seen that participation in the community is such a dramatic part of the process that you cannot skip it. Going to services allow you to become familiar with what community participation is and also helps you get a feel for how the congregation in particular expresses worship and enjoyment of G-d. Services are pretty straightforward as the rabbi usually guides you through the process fully. Everyone is in the same boat as you when it comes to what page to turn to next so there is no reason to feel awkward. People are going to be curious and friendly, enjoy that and be friendly back.

I would actually back up a bit though and say before you attend service you should attend a Jewish class first. I was weird and decided to become Jewish without ever meeting one. Most of you probably have some connection to Jewish people, but if you are like me it's good to get your feet wet through a Judaism: 101 class or two. I live in a college town with a small Jewish community. This means that there are no conversion classes at the synagogue but there is a Judaism 101 class at the college. Many synagogues do have introduction classes designed for non-Jews. So, before you ever think of knocking on the rabbis' door make sure to explore these options first.

Why is this important? Well do you really want to walk in and get disappointed that no animal sacrifice happened? I didn't think so. You should know what it is you are doing. Judaism 101 classes give history, culture and perspective. If you are intrigued *then* you should begin attending services. If you like the services *then* you should begin talking with the rabbi. Understand that, surprisingly, lots of people ask the rabbi to convert them. This includes people who want to marry Jews, people who have Jewish family or maybe only a Jewish father, people who have been coming to the synagogue for years and people who have just walked in the door for the first time. Conversion is an intimate and intense experience. The education is vast and time is needed. A lot of time. The rabbi may already have a full plate. So, I suppose the very first thing to consider is that this might take a while. You are not going to walk in and then walk out Jewish. Patience and understanding will help you avoid so much emotional difficulty. Don't see this process as something you need to finish. Recognize that becoming Jewish is redesigning your life and there is no time limit. Don't take ten years though.

What should you learn? Everything. But don't run off and delve into books and come back a year later expecting to knock the socks off of the rabbi with your vast knowledge. Trust me when I say that everything you can possibly learn from books will pale in comparison to even the shortest discussion of a single Torah portion with an enthusiastic rabbi. I think if I went back and tried this again I would approach it by learning *with* my community and rabbi rather than trying to cram it all in at once.

Hebrew is best learned with others and don't mimic the prayers. Learn the prayers through practice and understanding. There are prayers today that I have no clue what they mean but I can recite them. That is pointless. Hebrew comes to you as you learn how the words sound and what they mean. My synagogue did not have classes for a long time so my only option felt like books, but I did not ask other Jews to help me either. I thought that if I showed up already prepared it would be more impressive. I found that learning with others was far more meaningful.

I would strongly recommend finding and attending discussion groups, choirs and any other social activity available to you. Some of the most significant learning experiences I had came from Yiddish choir and Talmud study. It also helps to understand what it is you think you want to do. It's so easy to romanticize it all in your head and books and the internet reinforce this idea of what being Jewish can be. You just never know for sure until you experience Jewish life with other Jewish people.

When a Jewish person invites you to dinner, go. Put aside insecurities and shyness and recognize that social interaction is amazing in this community. Just go and experience. You are creating your network of Jews to turn to for every conceivable life experience you will encounter. You will make friends and may even find a family you didn't expect. You don't need to constantly remind them you are not Jewish, trust me when I say they know, but don't assume you are Jewish either. I think my demands that I was-too Jewish was what turned a lot of people off to me before they ever got to know me.

Jewish identity develops over time. When you get saved as a Christian you walk out that very night and self-identify as a Christian. When you convert to Judaism you do change status during the time in-between, but you are not Jewish until you actually convert. This is important. I am fairly certain I made this clear. You are in a new state of being, don't forget that. Being a Ger means you are learning how to be a Jew and that is different than being a Gentile. You are preparing your life to be a Jewish one which means practice and more practice. Just don't try to do it yourself. Let your rabbi and your Jewish friends and family guide you through it. Having Shabbos dinner with my Jewish family taught me so much. It built my identity and helped me practice far better than anything I ever tried by myself.

Do you really go around calling yourself a Ger? I suppose if you want to, but I would honestly say the best option is to think of yourself as a person learning how to be Jewish and use that as your title. You are learning how to be Jewish. No amount of emotional passion or fortitude is going to impress other Jews to the point of bypassing the conversion to accept your status so just don't try. Over time they will see you as a Jew from your devotion and actions and your conversion will make it official and solidify that.

A friend of mine who is converting refers to his religion on his Facebook as "Noahide converting to Judaism." This about covers it. Noahide is a Gentile who, like Noah who was not a Jew, follows the 7 Noahide laws for Gentiles. This person is not a pagan, is monotheistic but just isn't Jewish. I envy his decision. I just put I was a Conservative Jew years ago and never changed it. When I converted officially it would have been nice to have changed my status.

What do you do if you live 100 miles from the nearest synagogue or Jew? Well, consider moving. I don't mean to be a jerk about it, but did you not learn anything from me? You can't Jew without other Jews! I know this isn't easy or possible for lots of people but you must consider why being Jewish is so important to you and then figure out how you plan to live a Jewish life when you do convert. Conversion works so much better when you have a Jewish place to go to on a regular basis and can truly immerse yourself in the Jewish life cycle. Once you convert do you really want to go back to being alone without a Jewish community? I honestly believe that a person has to be willing to completely change their life for this choice. Find Jews.

Don't abandon your family. Even if your family is strongly religious and disapproves, don't try to escape them. Part of making this decision is fighting hard to embrace it fully. That is your strength and your choice and your family may never accept it, but at least give them a chance to. You don't have to shove it at them or make them see and hear it, but you should be open with yourself as much as possible. When a child makes the choice to change their religion oftentimes the family feels they are being abandoned or rejected. Depending on the religion they hold, they could even believe they are losing you forever. Staying open about what it is you are doing will help them see you are choosing something to make yourself happy and not something they should fear.

Don't try and do it all at once. If you try to weed out all the cotton/linen clothes you own, throw away non-kosher foods and try to buy a new set of pots and pans in the first week you will feel absolutely overwhelmed. Take each step one at a time. Experience each holiday as it happens and learn from it slowly. Wade in and feel everything and ask questions. You really don't have anything to prove and rushing won't help.

Finally, keep one thing for yourself for after your conversion. I began wearing a kippah every day, ate mostly kosher, had a mezuzah on every doorframe, had all the Jewish books everyone else had, worn tzizt, a tallit and tefillin before I ever entered the mikvah. I called myself Jewish for so long that most non-Jews were genuinely shocked to find out I just became Jewish recently. I wish I had kept something aside to do when I became truly Jewish as a way to make that transition more special. Like my Facebook religious status, it would have had a special meaning to me. Make sure you hold something to side that you just never do until your conversion is complete. Then embrace that one thing as incredibly special every day after.

Conclusion

How do I prepare you for your life-changing decision? I think I've made it pretty clear that I cannot. No one can. No book or online article or YouTube video is going to give you the secret to becoming a Jew. You just have to do it. You have to live it every single day and you have to allow other Jews to adopt you and show you the way. They probably don't know the way either as neatly as we would like, but by their example you will see what it means to be a Jew.

I did not become a Jew by reading a book (notice that I mention that bit at the end of mine.) I became a Jew because I allowed Judaism to take me in and reform who I was. I fought for a long time to force Judaism to submit to my will and in the end I was just trying to change the direction of the ocean by splashing frantically. Judaism is so deep and so immense that it cannot adapt for you. You have to wade in, try and not drown and take in as much as you can in the very short amount of time you have to do it in.

Do I really think it will take 10 years? No. You'll never be finished. You will always be growing in Jewish learning and development. After you buy all of the artifacts and books and after you get familiar with the holidays enough to be bored with them you will still find more Judaism you don't know. You must keep trying to become a better Jew.

I do think there is a maturity and patience; however, that changes the perspective of things. When I first read that conversion could take a year or longer I almost tossed the whole thing out the window. Little did I know... But it does take time to integrate into what is literally a new ethnicity. It is a people and a history and so much more than changing how you view G-d and your life.

Your rabbi will give you a timeline but don't rush. If I could advise you on any one thing it would be to not rush. Don't hurry through the books or the activities. Don't rush the prayers or force yourself to memorize anything. Don't get in a hurry to get your papers. Walk into this as though it might take you 10 years to complete and be emotionally ok with that. If you can approach this with reverence and respect you will understand that a single lifetime is not enough. Generations of Jews have built on top of each other since G-d gave us the written and oral law. You are adding a brick to a massive and towering wall and you need to take your time climbing up to place it.

Enjoy this. Let your rabbi know that you want to experience this, not just graduate. Don't let him or her try and get it done and over with. If you receive your conversion papers and go off into your life without really

תעודת גרות

On the 15th day of June 2015 corresponding to the 5th day of Tammuz 5775 according to the traditional Hebrew calendar at Congregation B'nai Sholom in Huntington WV Chad Greene entered the historic covenant between God and the people of Israel. Of his own free will he has made the following declaration:

I make this affirmation as I enter the eternal covenant between God and the Jewish people, the children of Israel. I choose to become a Jew of my own free will. I accept Judaism to the exclusion of all other religions, faiths and practices and now pledge my loyalty to Judaism and the Jewish people under all circumstances. I promise to establish a Jewish home and participate actively in the life of the Synagogue and the Jewish community. I commit myself to the pursuit of Torah and Jewish knowledge. If I am blessed with children, I will rear them as Jews.

Signature of Ger

Therefore, with the sanction of those whose names are signed below, Chad Greene was received into the community of the Jewish people and faith and was given the Hebrew name Shai

Rabbi

Witness Witness

Your people will be my people, and your God my God

עמך עמי ואלהיך אלהי

embracing what it is you signed up for you will just be limiting your own joy. The true happiness in Judaism comes from submitting yourself to greatness beyond your ability to control.

For me, I asked G-d, in His own words, to let me be chosen too. It might take a while for you to get His decision back.

The conversion experience is meant to change you. You get a Jewish soul or your Jewish soul ignites or maybe you just explore a new way to think of spirituality. Whatever you believe conversion does to you the point is that it changes you forever. That change is so impactful that you need a year to prepare for it. The ritual, the public welcoming – all of it is designed to make your birth into this new life easier.

Don't take it lightly. Don't skim and don't ask '*am I there yet.*' Allow yourself to become part of the process and guide it with your own will and your passion as it grows. We are all trying to truly be the Jews G-d wants us to be. You just have a bit of a late start, but you'll get there.

Photos

So yes, this is me in my fancy-schmancy Chanukah t-shirt next to a Christmas tree.

I told you. :/

My friends never cease in their joy of finding Chanukah themed items for me.

I think this was a birthday present actually...

And here is another Chanukah themed gift.

Napkins. They managed to find Chanukah napkins of all things.

Happy Happy Chanukah to me.

I made that kippah by hand. I loved that kippah. Look how gansta I am!

MUJSA Rabbi Days! That is me in the corner...not the fuzzy picture.

Here is me and the MUJSA gang at AIPAC 2014!

This is actually us headed for the airport to go home which was the only time I could get them all in a row and stand still at once.

My Yiddish Choir family!

From left to right is...everybody!

I'm tall so I hide...I mean, stand, in the back. See. I'm right there.

Sukkot on campus! The whole congregation came, the Yiddish choir sang and no one thought to take pictures until it got dark out.

oy.

The joke is that since I take the pictures there is no proof I really exist.

So Left to right is Temple Pres: Diane Shattls, Me, Rabbi Jean Eglinton and Ronni Fox-Glaser (of Ronni fame!)

Here is me at my first AIPAC with the MUJSA (toldja we were small!)

I was in a building with 6,000 Jews that year. Totally oy-some!!

Here is me and my best shiksa Christina at the first Israel Independence Day in Huntington WV (2011)

And finally, my Jewish family!

This is Norman Glaser, me and Ronni Fox-Glaser!

Left to right are my boys: Freddie, Moshe and Morticae (not Jewish)

This is me on my conversion day! ...Well a reasonable representation.

We did everything on Shabbat so no pictures!!

But, meh...close enough.

Extras

Because I am such a nice guy I have devoted this section to some basics for you and a handy-dandy reference for further reading.

Holidays

Chanukah

Chanukah is the Jewish Christmas. We've been over this.

Rosh Hashanah

Rosh Hashanah is Jewish New Year. We celebrate our own special new year even if most stores put out Rosh Hashanah cards in December.

Rosh Hashanah is the anniversary of the creation of Adam and Eve and we eat apples dipped in honey to wish for a sweet new year.

This part of the High Holy Days where you get to see all the Jews you never see any other time of the year.

Funny story: I got Yom Kippur and Rosh Hashanah confused my first year and I tried fasting from day one til Yom Kippur and almost gave up on this whole Jewish thing because I decided that was just crazy. This included not bathing because I read somewhere Jews don't bathe during this time.

Yom Kippur

Yom Kippur is the holiest day of the year. From an Orthodox perspective, this is a day where we "afflict" our souls as a way to obtain forgiveness for the previous year. Small print: You cannot get forgiveness from G-d for what you do to other people – you have to go ask them for forgiveness. They are serious ya'll.

Your first Yom Kippur is likely to be miserable. It's a remarkably deep and significant holiday, but if you just wander in after not eating you are going to find yourself sitting with a prayer book in Hebrew for like 6 solid hours. I only tell you this because you do not simply "do" Yom Kippur. This is an important holiday to prepare for because if you can appreciate the significance you will really enjoy the depth and ritual. If you are just curious you'll be bored out of your mind and too embarrassed to leave or even get up to pee.

I decided to be brave one time and attend the Orthodox Yom Kippur service 45 minutes away and interpreted the whole purity aspect to mean I needed to wear all white. When I arrived and found every single person in black suits and dresses…well, awkward.

Inside secret: Rabbis tend to be disappointed in potential converts who skip this major holiday. If you can study for it first and last the whole service it'll get you some bonus points! *wink

Sukkot

Every single one of my friends think this holiday is pronounced "suck-it." It's more like "Soo-kote" This is like our Thanksgiving! Actually, it is said that the Pilgrims looked in the Bible and found Sukkot which inspired Thanksgiving.

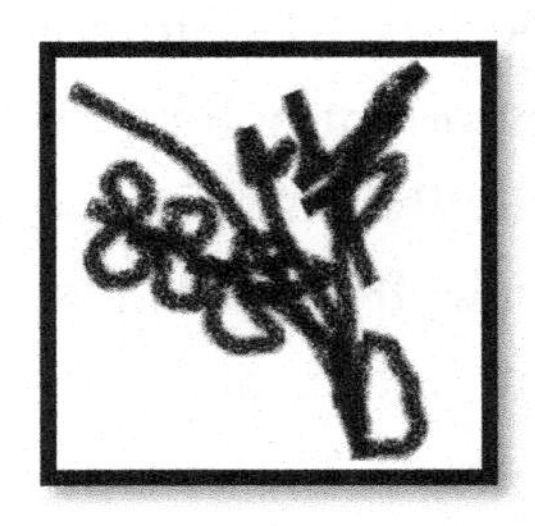

Sukkot is a very happy and joyous celebration that happens after Yom Kippur. It is a harvest festival and it marks the time when Jews lived in the desert for 40 years after the Exodus and lived in tent. Jews built Sukkahs (tents) and eat dinner in them. Orthodox Jews live in them for the whole holiday!

I, naturally, read about Sukkot online and decided to sleep in an actual tent (not a proper Sukkah) in my backyard for a week. I was very proud of my Jewish dedication.

Purim

Purim is often described as the "Jewish Halloween."

Kinda. We do dress up in costumes and get drunk! It is actually the holiday around the book of Esther which doesn't mention G-d even once. It is a story of an evil guy trying to kill the Jews and the brave Esther saves the day.

Yes, I mean we really get drunk.

Funny story: I once significantly confused all of my friends and coworkers when I told them I would be singing in a Purim play at the synagogue and they heard "Porn Play."

Simchat Torah

Simchat Torah is when we start reading the Torah all over again! A unique aspect of Jewish practice is that we all – every Jew on Earth – reads the same Torah portion at the same time. We repeat the entire

Torah once per year. I don't have any funny stories about Simchat Torah.

Tu B'Shevat

This one is about trees. Yes. I don't know either. Chabad.org says this is "New Year's" for trees. It really says that.

To my knowledge none of the Jews I know do anything for this holiday but apparently, many Jews eat lots of tree-bearing fruits that would naturally grow in Israel like dates, figs, grapes and pomegranates. Jews seriously dig pomegranates by the way. They are said to have 613 seeds (613 commandments) and they appear in Jewish artwork everywhere. All this time I just thought it was a fruit juice fad!

Passover

If you went to Sunday School then you know about Passover (Pesach). Besides the fun parts about frogs and rivers of blood we have a very in-depth and lengthy Seder that involves reading, singing, praying and many fascinating rituals. Also, it involves a lot of good food (once you get past the bitter herbs portion.)

This is an intimidating holiday because unless you have a family you will ultimately be invited to someone else's house which means eating a very large meal for several hours with lots of strangers. Don't worry though, unless said family is Orthodox most of the Jews there will be just as lost as you on the prayers and what gets dipped in what next.

Shavout

Shavout is when Moses received the Torah. It's kind of a big deal, right? You'd think so. Well in Israel it is. But in general Jewish areas, eh, not so much. I do not for the life of me know why. I am generalizing but at least in my area no one gets particularly excited about the one event that literally created our entire people.

My Jewish family introduced me to this holiday and it is a night of learning and discussion about the joys of Torah. Of course, there is food too. There is always food.

Jewish Items

Kippah

By now you know my infatuation with the kippah or yarmulke. To me it is such a vital accessory for a Jew to remind him or herself about their dedication to G-d. It immediately identifies you as a Jew and it also identifies you as observant.

Both boys and girls wear them, but normally boys do. You don't have to wear it all of the time like I do and many Jewish men do not. Many only wear a kippah during prayers or in synagogue.

Synagogues usually have a box full of community kippahs but I have always preferred my own. They can be any color, any fabric and have any design on them. Just remember that if you wear one in public people will assume you are Jewish and...well you saw how that worked out for me.

Mezuzah

A Mezuzah is a little wooden, metal, plastic or glass box you put on your doorway. You are probably familiar with this with Jewish homes. Deuteronomy 6:4-9, 11:13-21 commands us to place said verses on the doorposts of our homes so each box contains a handwritten scroll of the verse.

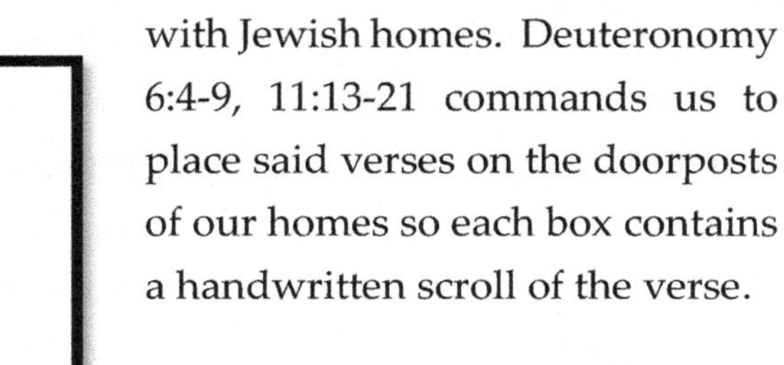

You put them on all the doorways of your home so most Jews have many of them. This is one of those commandments that really solidifies you to the Jewish faith. When you physically nail something to your house it means business!

Tallit

This is a very personal item and is usually worn only by men but many women wear them as well. The tallit is worn during morning prayers. Most synagogues have public-use ones to use.

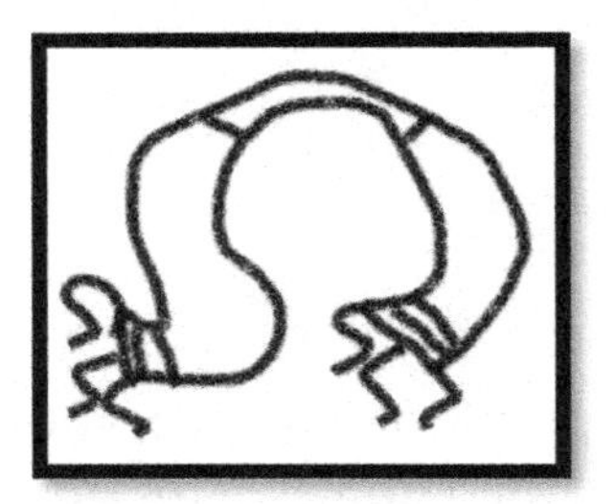

This is one of those serious items that for me required my conversion to feel comfortable using but your rabbi may want you to practice with one to get used to it.

It isn't something you usually buy for yourself as it is normally given as a gift at your Bar or Bat Mitzvah. But for converts usually a close Jewish friend or the synagogue gives you one.

Tefillin

Tefillin is another item usually associated with men and prayer but women can use it too. You adorn the head piece and wrap the leather strap around your arm and then you pray in the morning.

Tefillin is expensive and is usually a generational type thing. You have one for life in most cases. If you are serious about praying every morning then this is a good investment.

Shabbat Candles

Shabbat candles are a must for every Jewish household! Traditionally women pray over them to bring in Shabbat, but men can do it too. You light the candles and then you don't put them out. They are meant to glow throughout Shabbat evening.

I have found them to be remarkably soothing and spiritual. The physical act of initiating what will come anyways and honoring the moment is significant to me. White candles will do fine.

Havdalah Candle

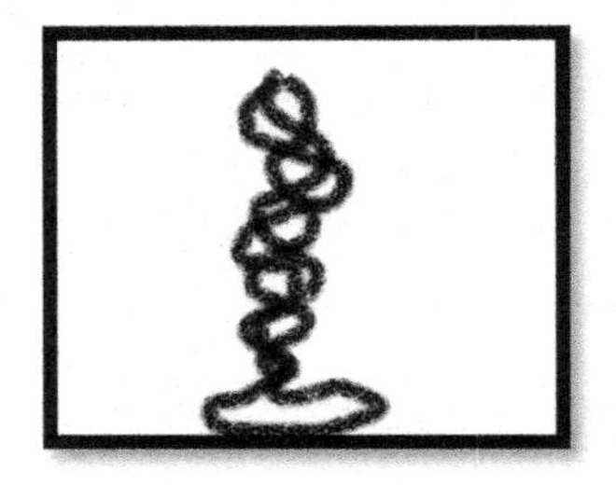

The Havdalah candle ends Shabbat. The candle is woven and colorful but it is also sad because Shabbat is leaving us. Men and women can light this candle and it is just part of the Shabbat ritual for every Jewish household!

Kiddush Cup

A Kiddush cup is essential for Shabbat prayers. Normally any male who has been Bar Mitvah'd will have his own Kiddush cup and will say the blessings. The cup is filled with wine or grape juice until overflowing and it shared in smaller glasses with everyone at the table.

This is usually an item given as a gift as well and is used throughout your lifetime.

Challah

Challah, with or without rabbi included, is an essential for Shabbat as well. You pray, cut the bread and salt it before your meal. Challah is something you can buy at stores that carry kosher items. But you can make it yourself as well.

Tzitzit

Of the commandments, this one is the most fascinating to me. It is optional because it requires wearing a four-cornered garment. But it is a positive commandment which allows you to choose to wear it and it symbolizes the 613 commandments. It is meant to be a reminder to think of G-d all day. The strands at the end are like tying a string to your finger to remember.

The garment is very strictly made however and has many detailed rules. It is awkward to wear if you choose to, but it has such simple yet significant meaning. I have purchased them online. Since Orthodox wear them like underwear they aren't very expensive.

Essential Reading

The Book of Jewish Values: A Day-by-Day Guide to Ethical Living by: Joseph Telushkin (ISBN-13: 978-0609603307)

Jewish Literacy Revised Ed: The Most Important Things to Know About the Jewish Religion, Its People, and Its History by: Joseph Telushkin (ISBN-13: 978-0061374982)

Jewish Wisdom: Ethical, Spiritual, and Historical Lessons from the Great Works and Thinkers by: Joseph Telushkin (ISBN-13: 978-0688129583)

Living a Jewish Life, Updated and Revised Edition: Jewish Traditions, Customs, and Values for Today's Families by: Anita Diamant (ISBN-13: 978-0061173646)

Choosing a Jewish Life: A Handbook for People Converting to Judaism and for Their Family and Friends by: Anita Diamant (ISBN-13: 978-0805210958

The Jewish Home: A Guide for Jewish Living by: Daniel B. Syme (ISBN-13: 978-0807408513)

To Life: A Celebration of Jewish Being and Thinking by: Harold S. Kushner (ISBN-13: 978-0446670029)

The Jewish Study Bible: Featuring The Jewish Publication Society TANAKH Translation (ISBN-13: 978-0195297546)

What is a Jew? By: Morris N. Kertzer (ISBN-13: 978-0684842981)

To Pray As A Jew: A Guide To The Prayer Book And The Synagogue Service by: Hayim H. Donin (ISBN-13: 978-0465086337)

To Be A Jew: A Guide To Jewish Observance In Contemporary Life by: Hayim H. Donin (ISBN-13: 978-0465086320)

The Jewish Book of Why & The Second Jewish Book of Why (2 volumes in slipcase) by: Alfred J. Kolatch (ISBN-13: 978-0824603144)

The Chumash: The Stone Edition, Full Size (ArtScroll) (English and Hebrew Edition) The Torah: Haftaros and Five Megillos with a Commentary Anthologized from the Rabbinic Writings by: Nosson Scherman (ISBN-13: 978-0899060149)

Essential Judaism: A Complete Guide to Beliefs, Customs & Rituals by: George Robinson (ISBN-13: 978-0671034818)

Settings of Silver: An Introduction to Judaism by: Stephen M. Wylen (ISBN-13: 978-0809139606)

Israel

Start-up Nation: The Story of Israel's Economic Miracle by: Dan Senor (ISBN-13: 978-0446541473)

Myths and Facts: A Guide to the Arab-Israeli Conflict by: Mitchell G. Bard (ISBN-13: 978-0971294561)

The Case for Israel by: Alan Dershowitz (ISBN-13: 978-0471679523)

Saving Israel: How the Jewish People Can Win a War That May Never End by: Daniel Gordis (ISBN-13: 978-0470643907)

Websites

www.chabad.org
Chabad.org is an Orthodox/Chassidic website with a remarkable wealth of information on all things Jewish and religious.

www.jewishvirtuallibrary.org
The Jewish Virtual Library holds an extensive history of Israel as well as many resources for Jewish life and practice.

outreachjudaism.org
Outreach Judaism is a fantastic resource for understanding the Jewish answer to Christian evangelism. This is Rabbi Tovia Singer's website.

www.standwithus.com
Stand With Us is a great resource for all things Israel. Their primary goal is to help college students battle anti-Israel bias.

http://urj.org
The Union of Reform Judaism. This is a website devoted to all things Reform Judaism and the Reform synagogues that connect with them.

www.uscj.org
The United Synagogue of Conservative Judaism. This is a resource for Conservative Judaism and congregations.

www.jewishfederations.org
One of the largest Jewish charities helping Jews across the world.

http://honestreporting.com
Honest Reporting provides accurate and reliable information on Israel and media bias.

www.aipac.org
The American Israel Public Affairs Committee is the largest lobbying organization for Israel in the U.S.

Notes

[1] My conversion date was 06/13/2013.
[2] Typical conversions take 1 to 2 years of study with a rabbi.
[3] There is no "Jewish sentence structure" but culturally one finds a similar pattern of speech which is often used in humorous ways in writing.
[4] A Kippah (Hebrew) is a small skullcap which can be worn by both Jewish men and women of various denominations to indicate both a Jewish identity and to show respect for G-d. This is also known as a Yarmulke (Yiddish.)
[5] See Chapter 4: Chanukah Oy Chanukah for more on this. Oy.
[6] Conservative, Orthodox and Reform are a few of the major Jewish religious movements. They indicate levels of observance, practice and belief.
[7] Christianity does include the books of the Tanakh (referred to as the Old Testament by Christians) and many believe Judaism to be intricate into Christian mythology. Islamic mythology also includes most Jewish prophets and historical characters as well. While the three religions did spring from the same source they are dramatically different today in practice and belief.
[8] *Choosing a Jewish Life: A Handbook for People Converting to Judaism and for Their Family and Friends* by: Anita Diamant 1998
[9] Jewish conversion is a controversial topic as an Orthodox Jew may not recognize a conversion performed by a Reform rabbi.
[10] I'm really a nice guy, just honest and blunt.
[11] Like this!
[12] Many Jewish converts report feeling strongly Jewish from childhood on and attribute this to a supernatural explanation. If you do not fit into that category, don't worry as many converts don't either. Sometimes finding Judaism is a very natural and inquisitive thing.
[13] In Christian mythology Jesus travels to Jerusalem and is said to have studied with the rabbis there. Christian bible: John 7: 14-24.
[14] The name of G-d should never be written on anything that can be easily erased and so a custom has evolved where you do not spell out G-d fully. Many use the name Ha Shem which means "The Name."

---

[15] It should be noted that in 1965 the Catholic Church declared all modern Jews should not be held responsibility for the death of Jesus in Christian texts and mythology. Many denominations of Christians still do blame Jews for the death recorded including the church I grew up in.

[16] There is a Christian sect known as "Messianic Jews" who, by all accounts, practice and believe in Evangelical Christianity but refer to themselves as Jews and practice Jewish customs. They are not typically included in a list of Jewish movements and are generally thought of as Christians. For more on this see Messianic Jews in Wikipedia.

[17] In 1995, a Christian rock/rap group, DC Talk, released an album titled *Jesus Freak*. This became a term of empowerment for Christians who were highly enthusiastic in their expression of faith.

[18] *Past Lives, Future Healing* by: Sylvia Browne 2001 audible book version

[19] I did research this but never discovered a Jacob Greene in the U.S Air force.

[20] The "three rejection" rule is more of a custom and some rabbis don't follow it at all.

[21] Many Jewish communities suffered anti-Semitism over the years and keep their doors locked and don't put out a sign. It is generally considered to be a very cautious thing to publically display a place and time where Jewish people congregate.

[22] My synagogue was built in the 1920's in an era when Reform Jewish congregations took on many customs of Christians including architecture and services. See Chapter 5: Conservative Conservative Jew.

[23] Animal sacrifices ended with the destruction of the 2nd Temple in Jerusalem.

[24] Conservative and Reform prayer books were written using both modern imagery of hope and peace as well as pieces from Tanakh like Psalms. It is often experienced in a call and response format everyone can follow along with, usually in English with some Hebrew.

[25] Judaism does not concern itself with the character Jesus or the mythology around him. It is unlikely you would hear anything about Jesus unless he was the topic of conversation in a lecture. See *Outreach Judaism* Rabbi Tovia Singer.

[26] Orthodox Jews are observant of Shabbat whereas Reform and Conservative Jews have varying levels of observance.

[27] This refers to the Oneg which is a social gathering after services that involves sweet treats such as cookies, cake and fruit.
[28] W.A.S.P. means White Anglo Saxon Protestant. It is a typical New England style description often associated with quiet and reserved Protestant Christians. My family belonged to such a culture but our religious expression was more lively...thus "a little bit of soul."
[29] This is not an official title but something many people are familiar with and they know what you mean when you say it. Essentially, as described, it refers to a person with no Jewish connection at all who insists on defining themselves as Jewish in public.
[30] It is true that within Jewish tradition once you convert you are supposed to be viewed as if you were born Jewish, this does not apply to the outside world.
[31] This word indicates a Jewish Witch. The person can be born Jewish or adopt Jewish practices and use this term. See: Willow from *Buffy the Vampire Slayer.*
[32] This is culturally true as many Jews do not view certain conversions as legitimate. Truthfully you only need a Beth Din (Rabbinic Court) and a rabbi to make you a Jew.
[33] This is true in the United States. In Israel is has been demonstrated that Orthodox Jews can nullify a conversion depending on their perception of its authenticity. This is not seen as in line with Jewish law by all Jews but is still done.
[34] Islam is the closest religion to Judaism as it is monotheistic whereas many consider Christianity to be polytheistic. The primary and mandatory belief Judaism prescribes is monotheism to our G-d.
[35] Kabalah is Jewish mysticism and is associated with the Zohar. Modern uses have turned it into a fad in recent years where is taken seriously by Orthodox Jews.
[36] Tzitzit is an undergarment shirt that is worn with fringes on each corner. Deuteronomy 22:12: "You shall make yourself twisted threads, on the four corners of your garment with which you cover yourself."
[37] Wearing tzitzit is a Jewish commandment that only applies to four countered garments and is partly to remind a Jew of his obligation to the Mitzvot or Commandments. It can only be worn in the daylight so you can see the fringes.
[38] Even though I am now a *real* Jew, I am still adjusting to this and many born Jews still insist on interrogating me as to my origins.

---

[39] Some Jewish conversions for men require a symbolic circumcision for those already circumcised.
[40] The High Holy Days include Rosh Hashanah and Yom Kippur. For more information please visit: http://www.chabad.org/holidays/jewishnewyear
[41] Passover is called Pesach and while acknowledged in some Christian traditions is completely unconnected to Easter. For more information please visit: http://www.chabad.org/holidays/passover
[42] *A Rugrats Chanukah* 1996 Season 4:ep 15
[43] A proper Chanukah Menorah has 9 candles with one used to light the others and is placed higher than the other 8. Please see: http://www.chabad.org/holidays/chanukah
[44] *The Chanukah Song* Adam Sandler 1995
[45] For more on Chanukah Celebrations: http://www.chabad.org/holidays/chanukah/article_cdo/aid/795380/jewish/Chanukah-Observances.htm
[46] The Chanukah Bush is actually fairly long lived for American Jews. In a 1959 appearance on The Ed Sullivan Show, actress Gertrude Berg mentioned having one. It essentially A Christmas tree with Jewish decorations.
[47] Blue and White are associated with Jewish celebration because they connect to the Israel flag which itself was designed to resemble the blue and white stripes on tallit.
[48] A dreidel is a small top. Each side of the dreidel bears a letter of the Hebrew alphabet: **נ** (Nun), **ג** (Gimel), **ה** (Hei), **ש** (Shin), which together form the acronym for "**נ**ס **ג**דול **ה**יה **ש**ם" (**N**es **G**adol **H**ayah **Sh**am – "a great miracle happened there"). http://en.wikipedia.org/wiki/Dreidel
[49] *The Hebrew Hammer* 2003: A comedy movie about Chanukah.
[50] Judah Maccabee: Hero in the story of Chanukah http://www.chabad.org/holidays/chanukah
[51] Christian Bible: John 10:22-39
[52] *The Origins of Reform Judaism* https://www.jewishvirtuallibrary.org/jsource/Judaism/The_Origins_of_Reform_Judaism.html
[53] Yiddish is a German language exclusive to Jews and is written with the Hebrew alphabet.

---

[54] *Reform Judaism*
http://en.wikipedia.org/wiki/Reform_Judaism_(North_America)
[55] *Why Advocacy is Central to Reform Judaism*
http://www.reformjudaism.org/why-advocacy-central-reform-judaism
[56] *Conservative Judaism*
http://www.jewishvirtuallibrary.org/jsource/Judaism/conservatives.html
[57] *Orthodox Judaism*
http://www.jewishvirtuallibrary.org/jsource/Judaism/Orthodox.html
[58] "You shall not round off the פְּאַת Pe'at of your head" (Leviticus 19:27) Payot: the hair in front of the ears extending to beneath the cheekbone, on a level with the nose (Talmud - Makkot 20a)
[59] New York style stereotype. Whiny, geeky, unnecessarily critical. Non-religious.
[60] *Fiddler on the Roof*, American musical comedy-drama, 1971
[61] Southern Christmas: think of a yard filled with every imaginable Christmas decoration available, multiple Christmas trees and decorations covering every square inch of the house.
[62] Chabad is a form of Chassidic Judaism. www.chabad.org
[63] A Joob is a new Jew, think "noob."
[64] Rabbi Tovia Singer is well known for his work in attempting to guide Jews away from their Christian conversion.
[65] Matisyahu is an Orthodox American reggae rapper and alternative rock musician.
[66] An example is The Maccabeats, an all-male a cappella group from Yeshiva University. Youtube "*Candlelight*".
[67] As in book of. Ruth said, "Intreat me not to leave thee, [or] to return from following after thee: for whither thou goest, I will go; and where thou lodgest, I will lodge: thy people [shall be] my people, and thy God my God: Where thou diest, will I die, and there will I be buried..." (Ruth 1:16)
[68] See Pre-Tribulation vs. Post-Tribulation Rapture as an example
[69] Painting: *Rabbis in a Debate* by B.Werner
[70] Shoah: Hebrew: השואה, HaShoah, "the catastrophe"
[71] At the time of this writing I currently only have one cat, Freddie. Both Morticae and Moshe have passed.

---

[72] *Dead Like Me*, 2003, is a TV show about randomly selected people who die and must build a new life with a new identity and take other souls as Grim Reapers.
[73] The Rebbe, Rabbi Menachem Mendel Schneerson (1902 – 1994) was the leader of the Chabad-Lubavitch and his authority on Jewish topics was respected by many,
[74] *What's That Thing on Your Head?* 2010 and my follow up *How's That Thing Stay on Your Head?* 2012
[75] Mashiach: The Messiah
[76] Jewish Feminism
[77] Sukkot is a festival that occurs after Yom Kippur and is comparable to Thanksgiving (There is theory Pilgrims looked to the Bible for a fall festival and adapted Sukkot.)
[78] For a *very* basic look: http://www.jewfaq.org/kashrut.htm
[79] Treif is a Yiddish word to describe any food that does not comply with the laws of kashrut.
[80] The Kosher Kitchen by Binyomin Forst ISBN-13: 978-1422608975
[81] Leviticus 18:22 just references men: "Do not have sexual relations with a man as one does with a woman..."
[82] Genesis 1:28
[83] *Occupation 101* is an award winning 2007 documentary reporting to tell the story of Palestinians being mistreated by Israelis. http://www.camera.org/index.asp?x_context=2&x_outlet=118&x_article=1415
[84] 2010: Operation Cast Lead
[85] Organizations like Honestreporting.com and StandWithUs.com provide information about this which includes tools and education to combat it.
[86] A full and accurate history can be reviewed here: https://www.jewishvirtuallibrary.org/jsource/israel.html
[87] http://www.thecaseforisrael.com/index.html
[88] http://www.cofi-wv.org
[89] *Ronni, The Little Jewish Girl Who Loved Israel* ISBN-13: 978-1466353015
[90] June/July 2014 Gilad Shaar, Naftali Frenkel and Eyal Yifrach Jewish teenagers in Israel (one American citizen) were kidnapped by Palestinians and later found murdered. Mohammed Abu Khdeir, an

---

Arab Israeli was found murdered in what appears to be retaliation by Jewish Israelis.

[91] http://outreachjudaism.org/

[92] Group of Rabbis or community leaders who decide if a convert is ready to officially convert.

[93] I poem I wrote in college circa 2005 or so.

[94] Isaac & Ishmael, Chabad.org http://www.chabad.org/library/article_cdo/aid/246646/jewish/Isaac-Ishmael.htm

[95] In 2013 Republican Senator Simcha Felder accused Democrats of intentionally putting off a vital vote he would not support until after the Orthodox Jewish Senator needed to leave to prepare for the Sabbath.

[96] In depth look at Slavery and the Torah http://www.chabad.org/multimedia/media_cdo/aid/1457459/jewish/Slavery-in-the-Torah.htm

[97] Glenn Beck hosted a remarkably inspirational event celebrating Israel in 2011.

Made in the USA
Coppell, TX
06 March 2022